Childhood

Key Concepts Series

CHILDHOOD

Michael Wyness

polity

First published in 2015 by Polity Press

Polity Press
65 Bridge Street
Cambridge CB2 1UR, UK

Polity Press
350 Main Street
Malden, MA 02148, USA

ISBN-13: 978-0-7456-6234-3 (hardback)
ISBN-13: 978-0-7456-6235-0 (paperback)

A catalogue record for this book is available from the British Library.

Library of Congress Cataloging-in-Publication Data

Wyness, Michael G.
    Childhood / Michael Wyness.
        pages cm. – (Key concepts series)
    Includes bibliographical references and index.
    ISBN 978-0-7456-6234-3 (hardback: alk. paper) – ISBN 978-0-7456-6235-0 (paperback) 1. Children. 2. Children–Social conditions. I. Title.
    HQ781.W958 2014   305.23–dc23
                                    2014016821

Typeset in 10.5/12 Sabon
by Toppan Best-set Premedia Limited
Printed and bound in the United Kingdom by T. J. International Ltd, Padstow, Cornwall

For further information on Polity, visit our website: politybooks.com

Contents

Acknowledgements

Some of the material in Chapter 2 draws on Wyness, M. (2014) Children, family and the State: revisiting public and private realms, *Sociology*, 48 (1): 59–74; Chapters 3 and 4 draw on Wyness, M. (2013) Global standards and deficit childhoods: the contested meaning of children's participation, *Children's Geographies*, 11 (3): 340–53; and parts of Chapter 5 draw on Wyness, M. (2012) Children's participation and inter-generational dialogue: bringing adults back into the analysis, *Childhood*, 20 (4): 429–42.

I want to thank my two boys Henry and Alec for their boundless optimism and energy in keeping me balanced when the pressures of work could easily have taken over. I also want to thank Beth for her love and constant support.

The work of some of my childhood colleagues at the University of Warwick needs to be acknowledged and my MA students have been influential in forcing me to clarify and extend my arguments on contemporary childhood.

Finally, I would like to thank Jonathan Skerrett of Polity for asking me to write this book and for his commitment to the project.

Introduction

The rise of critical theorizing within the social sciences at the end of the twentieth century has challenged many modernist bedrock concepts. Childhood is one such concept, which underpinned social scientific attempts at understanding, measuring and regulating the process of growing up. However, over the past two decades childhood has emerged as a contested concept, a cluster of critical and complex ideas around the nature of biological, social and psychological growth in the early years. The modernist conception of childhood formed through the theoretical and empirical work of developmental psychologists, and to a lesser extent functionalist sociologists, provided a hugely influential paradigm for the study of children and childhood. Children were viewed as incomplete social apprentices dependent on regulated support from more powerful adults as they progressed along a developmental pathway, carefully negotiating the appropriate stages as they reached the required biological age. Childhood was also underpinned by a range of political and institutional structures and developments in the latter half of the twentieth century, which focused on the regulation of childhood. The childhood studies developed in the late 1980s offer theorizing and research on children and childhood which challenges these earlier 'modernist' arrangements. At the same time, this research picked up on major social and political changes by both reflecting and shaping the changing nature of adult–child relations and the revisioning of childhood in the twenty-first century. This book will explore this new theorizing and research, setting out a much more complex and contested terrain within which academics, policy makers and practitioners understand and work with children and the concept of childhood.

We can take the example of Malala Yousafzai, a Pakistani girl who from the age of eleven started writing a blog for the BBC on the difficulties that Pakistani girls have gaining access to regular schooling, and who achieved global recognition at the age of fourteen after being shot by the Taliban for speaking out against their policies on women and education. Malala has become a representation of the desires and commitments of children, particularly girls, in less affluent parts of the world, as they strive for the same resources and opportunities as their more affluent peers in the West. She is also feted as a young heroine both at home and abroad in the way she embodies the agency of children in the twenty-first century who understand their social contexts and make a difference both locally and globally. From the example of Malala, we can distil three critical inter-related themes which form the basis of ongoing debate within childhood studies and are the focal points of the book; children's agency, the relationship between children, childhood and globalization and structural approaches that locate children within generational orders. Discussions of children's agency give prominence to social and cultural rather than biological factors, with the latter arguably limiting our understanding of children's agency. Hitherto, agency has been viewed as a property or disposition that children acquire once they have successfully progressed along a developmental pathway into adulthood. Childhood studies have rejected this developmental approach in favour of recognizing children's capacities as agents very early on in childhood. Agency in many ways has become a given within this research field, particularly within the sociology of childhood. Researchers have drawn on children's agency as a central conceptual device for analysing children's activities in a number of disparate contexts, from young children exercising choice on a routine basis over the food consumed within families through to the economic responsibilities that

Brazilian children have in communities that rely on child labour for their survival (O'Connell and Brannen 2014; Pires 2014). Children are assumed to have the capacity to make a difference within their social environments and this forms the basis of our examination of agency in Chapter 1. The paradigmatic status of agency is also evident across a range of other disciplines within childhood studies. In this chapter I discuss the multi-disciplinary potential of childhood and agency within the disciplines of history, anthropology and geography. While there is considerable analysis of children's agency from a number of different academic disciplines, there is much less on how children themselves view their capacities and agency. In the final part of this chapter I discuss children's own conceptualizations of their agency, particularly with respect to their status and levels of participation within school.

Agency has also been implicit in broader analyses of the twenty-first-century child in political and institutional as well as research terms, with concepts such as children's voice and participation becoming a more prominent feature of policy and practice agendas. In Chapter 2 I locate agency in broader political and institutional terms. A key theme here is change: in what ways has a changing political and social landscape underpinned a shift in the status of children and a reconceptualization of childhood? In what ways does policy and practice within child-related fields take more seriously the assumptions made within childhood studies that children are inherently agentic? Do social workers and teachers acknowledge children's agency by providing them with access to decision-making channels? I will address these questions in the first part of Chapter 2. While the bulk of the first two chapters focuses on researching the heightened profile of children as social agents in general, in the latter part of Chapter 2 I attend to the social distribution of children's agency. I introduce factors that differentiate children and childhood such as poverty, social class and age and in the process explore the differences in the way that different groups of children exercise their agency.

With reference to the second theme, globalization, one of the major shifts in theorizing within the social sciences in the latter decades of the twentieth century is the shift in frame of reference from national to global concerns. As with any aspect of social life, globalization has had a significant impact on our understanding of childhood and children's social relations. Globalization has had important consequences for children themselves, from the kinds of access that children have to schools, to their ability to engage in ever-more creative ways with a global mass media (Kenway and Bullen 2002). In the first part of Chapter 3 we explore the implications that globalization has for children in economic and political terms. In turning to childhood as a concept or social ideal in Chapter 3 our global connectedness in economic, political and cultural terms has had profound consequences for our understanding of children's lives. What globalization has done is to re-work the structure/agency debate by focusing on global and local issues. In the second part of Chapter 3 and in Chapter 4 we assess the way that childhood can be theorized in terms of a complex relationship between broader global trends and more localized factors. In the process we illuminate a different but parallel antinomy between a unitary model of childhood that emphasizes global uniformity and understandings of childhood that emphasize local diversity. One aspect of globalization is the attempt to generate a standardized model of childhood based on Western affluent world notions of childhood that include compulsory schooling and the development of 'individual' capacities. At the same time the attempts of Western nations and cultures to export this particular conception of childhood generate more critical localized constructions of childhood, with the accent on cultural diversity. While Chapter 3 explores a unitary or standardized global model of childhood, Chapter 4 focuses more on the cultural and political dimensions of globalization and the diverse ways that childhood is constructed at more national and localized levels. It also explores the diverse ways that children from very different political and cultural contexts draw on global media in developing their own identities.

In the final two chapters of the book the focal points are twofold: the position of children within the social structure and, more broadly, the status of childhood studies within the social sciences. In one important sense these two themes are related. The attempt to develop a corpus of theory that locates children and childhood at a more macro or structural level reflects attempts to establish 'childhood' as a dominant field of study within the social sciences. Chapter 5 focuses on theories that bring childhood in line with other sociological narratives on power, social difference and disadvantage. In exploring the position of children within the social structure, we outline generational approaches to the study of children and childhood. Thus, generation is advanced as a dimension of social stratification that can both complement and supersede more conventional narratives such as social class and gender. However, as with agency the concept of generation is contested. We tease out two approaches to the study of generational relations, the categorical and the relational. The former starts from a priori oppositional differences between 'child' and 'adult', making it easier for childhood scholars to compete with other social structural theorizing within feminism and Marxism. In effect, this approach assumes that the nature of children's lives and the kinds of societal forces on their lives are of a quite different order from the forces impinging on the lives of their parents, teachers and other adults, with adults nevertheless having power over children. An emphasis on action or agency as well as structure, on the other hand, generates questions about the role that children and adults play within these overarching theoretical structures and directs us towards more relational and inter-generational approaches. In setting out the possibilities of a generational approach to the study of childhood, I draw on a number of empirical cases. Thus, the problem of child abuse is subject to an analysis in generational terms, and the question is posed: to what extent are children at risk from abuse and maltreatment from adults due to their structural position within the generational order? We also illustrate the range of interdependent relations between children and adults from current representative research in the areas of children's participation and transnational migration.

In the final chapter we reflect on the position of childhood studies within two broader realms, the social sciences and the political public realm. We discuss the implications of a more interdisciplinary approach in researching children and childhood. The big research questions within the social sciences are now being addressed from a number of different disciplinary vantage points. Childhood is no exception to this trend. Arguably, the raison d'être of the new childhood studies is the shift away from a mono-disciplinary approach dominated by developmental psychology towards a more multi-disciplinary approach in order to provide broader and richer analyses of children and childhood. This chapter will attempt to move the debate further by exploring possibilities for a more interdisciplinary approach. It will weigh up the possibilities of an integrated disciplinary approach against a more default multi-disciplinary position where researchers from different subject areas tend to work in parallel. In illustrating interdisciplinary possibilities within childhood studies, I will discuss the concept of children's wellbeing, a much contested bundle of ideas but one that nevertheless invites commentary and analyses from a range of disciplinary vantage points. We draw on the examples of child labour and children involved in military conflict in exploring the potential for analysing children's wellbeing from a number of disciplines, including medicine, psychology, sociology and international development. In the final section of this chapter I will link this multi- or interdisciplinary focus to a parallel multi-agency approach in engaging with children within the public sphere. The chapter discusses the relationship between childhood studies and the policy and practice of working with children at political, institutional and professional levels. Thus, the *Every Child Matters* agenda is explored as a political initiative in England with a much stronger focus on supporting children and families through close ties between different 'welfare' agencies and professionals. We explore the parallels between scholars and professionals, both with a mandate to work more closely with children.

1
Conceptualizing Agency

Children's agency has become a direct challenge to hitherto dominant ideas on children's development that effectively define agency as a status assumed by children once they leave childhood. Moreover, a developmental focus on the acquisition of agency privileges biological and psychological factors over social factors. Thus agency has not only been associated with children when they leave childhood and enter adulthood, but biological and psychological growth towards this end point. In the first part of this chapter I explore recent work within the field of childhood studies where agency has achieved almost paradigmatic status. It has become a key assumption in analyses of children and childhood at local and global levels. In challenging the developmental and 'cognitivist' focus, empirical research has drawn on the concept of children's agency within a diverse range of social and cultural contexts, from UK-based children developing religious and spiritual agency through to Indian children of sex workers using their political agency to try to improve conditions for themselves and their families (Hemming and Madge 2012; Sircar and Dutta 2011). Children's agency has thus become an embedded feature of empirical research on children and childhood. However, within sociology, arguably the dominant discipline within childhood studies, there is some conceptual ambiguity over the nature of children's agency. In part this is due to agency's taken-for-granted status, a largely assumed conceptual starting point. The political and moral commitment to agency and its attractiveness as an empirical focus has led to the neglect of a more thorough theoretical grounding (Valentine 2011). A cursory conceptual inventory of the field identifies an individualist and romanticized strand of theorizing where thinking around children's agency represents the search for the unmediated adult-free voice of the child (Hart 1997; Franklin 1997). Within this framework children are often viewed as being constrained, exploited and controlled by parents, teachers and other adults. Children's agency is hidden, muted or marginalized as adults seek to regulate children's lives. This is set against an emerging social model within sociology where children's agency emerges from ongoing relations between children and adults (Oswell 2013). There is here a more positive inter-generational basis to children's agency. In the first part of the chapter I critically examine the individualist approach to children's agency from a social and relational perspective. The focus on agency here is on three dimensions: agency emerging from inter-generational relations; the embodied and emotional nature of children's agency; and its moral character.

In the second part of the chapter I go beyond sociological thinking and discuss the possibilities of the social nature of children's agency from other disciplinary vantage points including history, anthropology and geography (Rosen 2005; Montgomery 2008; Zeiher 2003). The popularity of children's agency for scholars from a range of disciplines within childhood studies offers further evidence of the shifting ontological and epistemological status of children and childhood. While adult researchers make certain assumptions about children's capacities and competence, rather ironically there is less evidence from children themselves as to what agency means to them. In the final section we discuss children's own conceptions of agency. Drawing mainly on their experience in schools, children provide a distinctive approach to agency in the way that they reflect on how they experience their schooling and understand the implications of having their agency recognized by teachers in school.

Conceptualizing agency

Agency is often assumed to reflect dominant Western liberal values of self-determination, rationality and independence

(Ling 2004; Boyden 1997). Moreover, these are normally seen to be characteristics of fully formed individuals or adults, with children aspiring to this status following carefully arranged and regulated developmental trajectories. Children are viewed as dependants until they grow into adulthood, with their social and moral development closely following their biological and psychological growth. Acquiring independent status, for example, implies that children develop through very specific cognitive stages. According to developmental psychology children move from an early sensory-motor stage where they engage with their environments using their senses to the much later 'formal operative' stage where in adolescence they view the world in more abstract rational terms. The latter is viewed as the embodiment of these Western values of rationality and independence with successful negotiation of these stages a precondition for acquiring agency (Burman 2007). A more recent strand of thinking on the relationship between childhood and agency within childhood studies has tended to ignore developmental thinking and view the child *as well as* the adult as the autonomous independent individual. In Chapters 3 and 4 we will discuss the limitations of this model in terms of globalizing processes. Here I want to focus on this individualist model of childhood and agency where there has been a shift from the individual autonomous adult towards identifying the conditions and the circumstances within which children can become autonomous individuals freed from the regulatory constraints of adults (Lee 2001). I want to pursue the analysis of agency here through a discussion of children's participation, which has both a theoretical and empirical significance, within the field of children's studies. We need to be careful not to conflate agency and participation (see Chapter 2). Nevertheless, it is usually assumed that children exercise agency when they participate. Participation has developed out of the UN Convention on the Rights of the Child (1989) and has come to mean 'children expressing their views freely and (having) them taken seriously' (Landsdown 2010, p. 11). Whether we are talking about children in the home, in school or in many cases in the workplace, agency here implies children having the capacity, the space and the opportunity to have some involvement in decision-making processes.

The individualistic strand of thinking has generated an over-romanticized conception of agency. This is evident in a number of ways. Firstly, there is a search for authentic forms of participation, particularly with respect to children's voices. For some the search for authenticity has become a 'fetish', an end at all costs (White and Choudhury 2007). Hitherto, it has been argued that adults have played a dominant, even overpowering role in children's lives (Kitzinger 1997). This argument is extended to participatory initiatives where ostensibly adult involvement and agendas are less prominent. The structuring and regulating of participatory initiatives by adults has led to critical commentary on the artificial and often tokenistic nature of children's involvement (Hart 2008). School councils, for example, are viewed as typical participatory initiatives found in most schools in the UK. They have often been criticized as having little power to advance children's interests, being limited to highly structured discussions about the 'charmed circle of lockers, dinners and uniform' (Baginsky and Hannam 1999, p. iii). Partly as a response to this, researchers and professionals are developing strategies for restricting adult influence from channels of communication within a number of institutional and social settings, granting children a degree of autonomy in articulating their interests from a genuinely child-focused perspective. In more institutional contexts this means that children have more agenda-setting powers, with adults in the background acting as facilitators. Pinkney (2011), for example, analyses children's voices in terms of relations that English welfare professionals have with child clients. One respondent, a children's rights officer, discusses the difficulties of uncovering the child client's 'pure' voice. Pinkney (2011, p. 41) goes on and speculates: 'an impure voice in this scenario might be one that was mediated, muffled, directed, coached, constrained or interpreted'. The 'purity' of the child's voice here is associated with the absence of adult involvement or the limiting of adults' interpretive powers. While there are issues with children's ability to speak for themselves, various authors have taken issue with this idea that the child's voice can ever be free from adult distortion or mediation (Thomas 2007; White and Choudhury 2007; Lee 2001). Children's voices are always mediated or arising out of ongoing dialogue with others.

Thus issues of authenticity merge with the search for the unmediated child's voice. This is children's agency that is not regulated; children's participation that is not compromised by the actions of adults. A dominant motif within childhood studies is the participating child in search of an authentic unmediated voice within a social and political space relatively free from adult intervention. Lee (2001) has questioned the idea of the child being able to acquire an unmediated voice. If we associate participation and voice with a move towards individual autonomy, then we are starting to see the autonomous adult as the benchmark from which assessments of the participating child are made. In other words, in searching for children's unmediated voice, we might want to focus on the ways in which adults are able to demonstrate this model of agency. This poses considerable problems. Lee (2001) argues that postmodern social theory of the past thirty years has focused on the 'incomplete' nature of adulthood. Adults have to rely on others in order to get their messages across; their understandings of the world are always mediated by other people and objects. The search for an authentic adult voice is seen as a fruitless task for it is always filtered through a range of media and resources. Thus the search for the authentic unmediated voice of the child must suffer a similar fate. In a complex media driven world both adults' and children's voices are heavily mediated.

Secondly, the difficulties in finding a pure form of voice and thus an authentic form of children's agency are also encountered when conducting empirical research with children. In particular, the search for authentic data from children within their own social contexts is often hampered by the role that adult researchers play in structuring the research process (Mandell 1991). The aim of many researchers here is to minimize their roles as adults within the research context so that researchers are in a stronger position to generate 'pure' unmediated forms of data from child respondents. Mandell (1991) in an early ethnography of young children's cultures in the playground attempts to play the 'least adult' role by trying to become a member of young children's peer cultures, by refraining from taking part in 'adult' activities and by trying to pass herself off as a 'friend' of the children. The search among ethnographers of childhood for an authentic or 'natural' child's voice has proved somewhat elusive and in some respects futile. Various authors have stressed the power differences between the researcher and the children in physiological, psychological and social terms (Mayall 1996; Thorne 1993). Thorne (1993, p. 17), for example, refers to the language that adults use when in contact with children either as guardians, teachers or researchers, which accentuates the power differential between them and the children. In her reflections on working with young children she comments:

> During one of my forays on the Oceanside playground, a boy came over and asked, 'What ya writing?'...I responded, 'I am writing down what you are doing. Do you mind?' He warily edged away. 'I didn't do anything' he said. Another of my early explanations – 'I'm interested in the behaviour of children' – also brought defensive responses. I came to see that verbs like 'doing' and 'behaving', which figure centrally in the social sciences and child rearing, are both practices geared to social control.

Thus the very language that adults take for granted when talking to children can act as a barrier to generating authentic child-focused data. These visible and invisible differences are major impediments to ethnographers trying to enter children's cultures and elicit children's authentic voices. In some respects, then, children's agency and voice are irrevocably mediated. Whether this must lead to children's agency being subsumed within adult regulatory frameworks is another question. An empirical response to this question from other ethnographers is that the immersion in children's social environments means embracing their roles as adults (Ahn 2010; Corsaro and Molinari 2008). In their research on peer cultures within playgrounds Corsaro and Molinari (2008) played the roles of incompetent adults which allowed them to get close to the children while at the same time giving the children the upper hand in terms of the way they were able to induct the researchers into the various peer groups. This methodological approach challenges the dichotomous relationship between the powerful adult and powerless child and directs us towards reframing the analysis of agency. Rather than trying to identify the child's voice unfettered by the regulatory powers of adults, we should be exploring the way that children's agency is enabled through the kinds of relationships that children have with their social environments (Lee 2001). We are arguing here for the quintessentially social nature of children's agency.

The social relational nature of agency is an emerging strand of thinking within the sociology of childhood. Mayall (2002, p. 21) argues that there are two components to agency: children are, firstly, social actors by virtue of their social being, they are full members of society. Secondly, 'action' is more fully developed into agency, in that children's actions make a difference within a wide array of social contexts.[1] This conception of agency is confirmed by Oswell (2013, p. 3): 'children are not simply beings, they are significant doings. They are actors, authors, authorities and agents. They make a difference to the world we live in'. Children as agents are immersed within the social world and thus embedded in relations within which they have a formative influence. The child agent is not only capable but also fully social. Agency cannot simply be equated with individual choice or individual autonomy (Valentine 2011), it needs to be viewed as a relational concept, an effect of complex shifting social arrangements. Corsaro's (2011) process of 'interpretive reproduction' emphasizes children's agency as a collective phenomenon. His empirical focus is young pre-school children who have agency in their capacity to create and sustain relations with their peers and thus generate a culture for children. Children within these cultures are meaning makers, they interpret the cues given by their peers and act accordingly in helping to reproduce the contexts within which children play and interact with others. From his observational data Corsaro (2011) identifies an ongoing tension between children playing together and the claims of other children to join the game being played. The latter is eventually able to find ways of joining other children in their play which both maintains and extends the game being played thus reinforcing the rules and acknowledging the interactive space of the other children. Children create and reinforce group rules in the process exercising their agency.

Children's agency is a concept that also emerges from the dynamic nature of inter-generational relations. Bjerke (2011,

p. 97) talks about the 'embedding of agency in intricate family relations'. Her sample of Norwegian children stresses the importance of being treated as 'differently equal partners' by adults, rather than having greater independence from adults when being involved in decision-making processes. Various researchers have also talked about agency in terms of children negotiating their religious identities and affiliations with their parents (Hemming and Madge 2012; Hopkins et al. 2007). Hemming and Madge (2012) talk about the different forms that these negotiations take, including children publicly conforming to their parents' faith while privately questioning it; children openly debating with their parents the issue of faith and in some instances children influencing their parents' religious affiliations.

A more inter-generational focus draws out the nuanced nature of agency and at the same time challenges a zero-sum conception of power. Children's voices are often heard and acknowledged through more interconnected relations between children and adults. One example of this is Hannah, a 13-year-old English girl with chronic health problems. Despite pressure from the local health authority, Hannah refused to have 'life-saving' heart surgery (Wyness 2012). One version of this story is the conflict between the incompetent child making a solitary life-changing decision and the expertise of the medical profession. However, in reality Hannah's agency was exercised through a supportive family network. Moreover, a local child protection officer took issue with the way that the hospital was trying to force her to have a transplant. Agency here is relational, arising out of inter-generational relations. Hannah's agency developed over time; not just in terms of any developmental logic, but in terms of Hannah living with her illness for most of her life and being in a position to make an informed contribution to decision-making processes on the nature and direction of her treatment.

While agency here could be construed as an effect of inter-generational consensus, its socially dynamic nature also suggests a more conflictual relationship between adult and child. Valentine (2011) extends the argument in that children's agency emerges from complex ongoing power relations between children and adults. She uses the example of the concept of children's vulnerability. She argues that children might view themselves or their peers as vulnerable and thus in need of protection from adults, which could be taken to challenge a researcher's view that children ought to have agency. They might also be exercising their agency in the way they articulate their awareness of the kinds of responsibilities that adults have towards children within a 'risk' society. Moreover, there is also an awareness of the difficulties that adults might have in discharging their responsibilities in the way that these protections might restrict children's use of physical and social space. Children are aware of the difficulties adults have when juggling the demands to keep children safe, while giving them the space to play and explore. Children here articulate the complexity of adult–child relations and also display rational acceptance of the possibility that sometimes children need to be constrained.[2]

This is a far more complex notion of agency: agency is not simply an autonomous space within which children are free to make choices; it is 'inflected with power'. Children are implicated within networks and hierarchies of power (Valentine 2011, p. 353). Thus children can modify adult power even when the adults are trying to redistribute their power. Gallagher (2008) discusses participatory research methods in terms of how he tried to 'empower' his research respondents, which sometimes backfired when his respond ents resisted these attempts at 'empowerment'. Ironically, children exercised power in the refusal to accept the power distributed to them by the researcher. While it is clear that the distribution of power 'downwards' is itself a reflection of wider power relations between adults and children, encounters with children within a research context generate points of resistance, which make the relationship between power and agency far more complicated.

Emotional and embodied agency

Agency also has to be seen as emerging from social relationships which are 'emotional, embodied and creative' (Mackenzie and Stoljar 2000, p. 21). There are two ways of thinking about the emotional nature of children's agency. First, agency is fully embodied in the way that human subjects reflect on their situations through what Archer (2000) refers to as a range of 'emotional clusters'. She argues that we routinely engage in inner dialogue with ourselves in the way that we experience, feel for and connect with others. These clusters of emotions are viewed as internal narratives on our concerns for ourselves and others; they relate to our ability to do things, our physical wellbeing and our sense of self. While Archer's work does not explicitly include children, there is nothing in her analysis that precludes children from having access to these emotional clusters. Children are able to reflect on their selves and others and able to articulate their feelings through a variety of modes of communication (Hunleth 2011). We can see elements of children's emotional agency in Udi Mandell Butler's (2009) ethnography of street children in Rio de Janeiro. One of his central concepts is *revolta*, a term used by many of his respondents which generates feelings and behaviour of rage and revulsion over the circumstances in which they find themselves on the street. It is also used by the children as a means of expressing their feelings about their home lives, which often act as motivating factors or triggers in moving out of the home and onto the street. Thus children express *revolta* in the way that they talk about the abuse and the poverty that they sometimes experience with their families. Here children are reflecting on their life-chances at an emotional level, as well as identifying an emotional state on the street that becomes a central feature of their social identities.

Secondly, we can explore the emotional nature of agency with respect to the ways that children's emotions do not always correspond to a top-down developmental model of children gradually acquiring forms of emotional competence and intelligence. Drawing on Ahn's (2010) observations of groups of pre-school middle-class American children, we can argue that young children use their emotions to generate alliances and hierarchies with their peers. Often this is done contrary to the expectations of the teaching staff. Children's emotional behaviour in Ahn's research did not always neatly correspond to age-related inner emotional states. Neither could it be seen simply as instances of deviant behaviour. Despite teachers' attempts to refer to inner emotional states such as sadness, anger and compassion, and how these emotions might be appropriately 'performed', children utilize their emotional agency through the relations they have with others in order to assert some sort of control within peer groups. Given the fragile nature of hierarchies within young children's peer groups and the ever present threat from adults that their play will be disrupted, children use their emotions tactically to gain some advantage within their peer groups. Drawing on Corsaro's (2011) 'interpretive reproduction', children appropriate adult meanings for their own social ends, which often conflict with adults' expectations.

Children's moral agency

A social conception of children's agency also incorporates a moral dimension. There has been little sense until recently that children had any moral agency. The conventional view has been that as part of children's social apprenticeship as children, they have to learn how to become moral agents, that is, as with social competence, children's capacity to make moral judgements and claims is recognized later when children leave childhood. Mayall (2002) goes further in arguing that in some respects morality here is linked to notions of responsibility and that children are expected to become responsible in terms of attitude and behaviour, for example, in the way that they are supposed to sit and listen to their teachers in class. At the same time these children are unlikely to be regarded as moral agents. Issues of reasonableness, respect for others and a capacity to empathize are central here with research supporting the notion that children from a very early age have these capacities (Mayall 2002, pp. 88–111). Moreover, these capacities are present in and through the relationships that children have with others. In Chapter 4 I discuss the global misrecognition of children's agency when associated with child labour. Wihstutz (2011) argues that the work done within the home, particularly where children have taken on responsibilities for care, highlights the moral agency of children. In her analysis of children caring for chronically ill parents in Germany, Wihstutz (2011) talks about children exercising their agency as a way of improving things for themselves and their families. Children are aware of the importance of caring for others, particularly family members, and conscious that their caring can make a difference to the wellbeing of others within the family and to the stability of the family overall. Moreover, these caring responsibilities become normalized over time. Agency here is related to children's ability to take responsibility for themselves and others (Wihstutz 2011). For some children there was a strong sense of reciprocity: children view the care that they bestow on their parents or caring roles that they think they might have to assume as they get older as simply being part of a family where all members care for each other (Mayall 2002, pp. 107–8).

Moral agency can take other forms. Thus in different cultures we can identify different criteria for making moral judgements. Issues of awareness of others and a set of rules around expectations and the rightness of behaviour are central to most systems of morality. Nevertheless, in Western cultures, the concept of responsibility is usually central to most moral considerations made by adults and children alike. Froerer (2011) in her analysis of Indian children's moral thinking argues that other criteria are equally important. Her ethnographic study focuses on the ways that Indian children impute moral accountability. Claims are made about the supernatural world. According to the children transgressive behaviour is punished by supernatural forces that render the transgressor incapacitated. Thus the children attribute the illness of other children to breaking moral rules.

The multi-disciplinary nature of children's agency

A social conception of agency emphasizes its embedded nature in the way that agency emerges from relationships and roles that children play in decision-making processes, in the work that they undertake and in the way that they interact with adults. Sociological theories thus emphasize the contexts and relationships within which children's agency is embedded. In turning now to other disciplinary approaches within the broader field of childhood studies, we can find social, moral and emotional elements in the work of historians, anthropologists and geographers with an interest in children and childhood.

Historical constructs and the political child

Much has been said about the socially constructed nature of childhood (Valentine 2011; James 2009). While it has become a theoretical orthodoxy within childhood studies, it has a more complex and ambiguous relationship with the concept of children's agency. On the one hand, the focus on the social rather than the biological gives us more opportunity to identify the different ways that children exercise their agency. The idea of childhood as a historical convergence of social and political forces opens up the possibility of identifying a diversity of distinctive forms of childhood. Just as societies take different forms over and across time, so do the contours of childhood adapt to these different social structures, offering the potential for children to be recognized in terms of agency. Children are limited by their biology but nevertheless children's social and political capacities belie their age and inexperience. Thus, in moving beyond developmental conventions, we can start to identify ways in which children are able to exercise a degree of agency. At the same time, constructionism has been more interested in the convergence of historical, political and social influences on the child, a focus on the role that adults play in shaping discourses on childhood. Ariès' (1961) historical analysis is seminal in providing a modern conception of childhood but the roles of children themselves are notably absent in this historical construction. Various others have followed suit in providing historical constructions of childhood (Turmel 2008; Rose 1992; Hendrick 1997). Far fewer have provided a social history of children and examined the contributions children have made in a number of spheres over time.

The concept of the political child is a useful way of drawing out the historical contributions made by children as agents. This concept is usually seen as a contradiction in terms. As Hannah Arendt, a famous critic of children's involvement in politics, argued, children are to be hidden within the private

sphere of 'natality, love and intimacy' where they are protected from the pressures of the public realm (Bethke Elshtain
1996, p. 14). Arendt was highly critical of the 'racial' deseg-
regation that took place in Little Rock schools in the USA in
the 1950s as it exposed children to the politics of race before
they were developmentally ready. In some instances children's
exposure to the 'external' world of politics is seen as a form
of political indoctrination with vulnerable children being
exploited by adults in the interests of political ideology. Conventional historical narratives thus exclude the political or
historical role of children. However, linking children's agency
to historical constructionism allows us to challenge this conventional viewpoint. Bethke Elshtain (1996), for example,
argues that the absence of children within these narratives is
at variance with a range of historical events and situations
where children have been highly political.

One way to think of the political child is to explore the
roles that children played in military conflict over time. David
Rosen (2005) examines the central role of children in military
conflict in a number of historical settings. Boys were regularly
signed up by the English army during the medieval period,
particularly during the Crusades. In the 1770s the English
army recruited children to suppress the insurgent American
rebellion in the war of independence. Similarly the rebel army
recruited young boys. Dann (1980) has written about Henry
Yeager, who signed up as a 13-year-old to fight for the rebel
army. He became a drummer boy for Washington and for a
while was arrested and sentenced to death by the British army
for espionage. The sentence was later commuted after he had
spent some weeks in prison. He was eventually captured on
board a rebel boat and spent a further two years in prison.
The Civil War in the USA in the 1860s was seen as 'a war of
boy soldiers' (Rosen 2005, p. 5) with historians estimating
that between 10 and 20% of combatants were children. In
the twentieth century children also played significant roles in
military campaigns in Palestine and in Central and Eastern
Europe. The latter was notable on two counts: many children,
despite the age restriction imposed by the British government,
routinely signed up to fight during World War I. In World
War II children played formative roles in Jewish resistance
movements challenging Nazi occupation in Eastern Europe.

While figures are estimates, around a third of all Jewish resistance fighters were aged between fifteen and twenty (Rosen 2005, p. 21).

Marson (1973) focuses on children's political 'industrial' potential in his account of the children's strikes of 1911. Working-class children from across more than sixty towns and cities in Great Britain left their classrooms and schools and marched on the street. Within a broader political context of industrial unrest, children demanded the ending of corporal punishment and a shorter school day. While the authority's responses were predictably punitive with strikers being labelled the 'truant class' and the 'ragged edge' of the school population, Marson (1973) refers to their agency in terms of their independence and their ability to organize and coordinate their movements across a number of local schools. There is thus an important social and collective dimension to children's agency here. This level of collective agency was also evident in the USA at the turn of the twentieth century, with children aged between eight and fourteen demonstrating entrepreneurial skills and some industrial muscle in their roles as newspaper sellers on the streets of New York. The 'Newsies' became a regular feature on the streets of New York selling newspapers (Woodhouses 2009). They had to buy the newspapers from the publishers and so they were under pressure to sell all their stock to ensure they made a profit on the street. Despite their popularity, their position on the street was tenuous. But they were a well-organized group who eventually formed their own union to protect their collective interests. In 1899 their union flexed its muscles in a dispute with the powerful Hearst and Pulitzer publishing empires who increased the cost of the newspapers. Their collective strength enabled them to strike, forcing the newspaper owners to climb down (Corsaro 2011).

If we move forward to the recent historical past – in the 1970s black South African children and young people were arguably at the forefront of the anti-apartheid movement. There was a rapid expansion of higher education in the 1960s, and young blacks were able to take advantage of this in becoming much more politically conscious of their situation. This consciousness took the form of an organized street protest in Soweto in 1976 with between 15 and 20,000 children and young people involved. Up to 200 schoolchildren were gunned down by government forces (Bundy 1987). The impetus here was the introduction of Afrikaans, the language of the white minority rulers, as a compulsory language to the curriculum. While there was some criticism of the role of adult leaders from the youthful political leaders, many children were highly politicized and engaged with the struggle to end apartheid, working alongside their parents (Ndebele 1995).

For some, the difficulty with children's agency is associating any form of voluntarism with children's actions (Kimmel and Roby 2007). Arendt (1959) saw children's involvement at Little Rock as a form of political indoctrination, with vulnerable children being exploited by adults in the interests of political ideology. And it is clear that the Holocaust made it almost impossible for children to make an informed choice about whether to participate. Thus, we may be struggling to discern any conception of agency here. Moreover, Denov (2012) cautions us against constructing the child soldier as a victim, an offender or a superhero. Notions of agency here are complex: on the one hand, the recruitment of child soldiers through coercion accentuates children's victim status; on the other hand, the various high-profile cases of war crimes committed by children reinforce their culpability and in one sense their agentic status.[3] Nevertheless, Rosen (2005) refers to the way that children and their families during the Holocaust saw the passive acceptance of death by the Nazis as a form of 'dishonour'. In many of these historical cases children were encouraged by parents and schools to take up arms, with their involvement seen as a moral duty. When referring to the work of Primo Levi, a Holocaust survivor, Rosen states that for child partisans involved in the resistance movement 'there is no doubt that even a child has moral agency' (Rosen 2005, p. 24). Historically, then, we have another example of children's agency as moral. Children here are often of their time and social context: they can neither be wholly protected from nor explicitly exposed to their circumstances; they are simply of their circumstances, as was the case of children and young people in South Africa: they were part of ongoing struggles that many communities face on a daily basis.

One possible way of moving beyond the conflation of agency with voluntarism is to differentiate levels of child agency. In an interesting article on the agency of child domestic workers in Tanzania, reference is made to 'thick' and 'thin' conceptions of agency (Klocker 2007). The latter derives from a complex series of constraining external factors, whereas in the former case children are able to act, have more space to make a difference within a much broader range of contexts. These forms of agency can be viewed as part of a continuum of circumstances and contexts within which children's agency can be 'thickened' or 'thinned', that is, children's agency is a dynamic and ongoing convergence of factors that change over time giving children more or less capacity to act as social agents. Oswell (2013) talks about thin conceptions of agency as forms of 'tactical agency': children using interstitial spaces, often hidden, and often in creative ways that temporarily subvert structures dominated by adults.

Anthropological approaches

As with other social sciences, anthropology in the past tended to make assumptions about children and childhood in terms of an absence of agency with a strong focus on the socializing powers of adults and community structures and the notion of the child as a transitional object going through the process of socialization (Froerer 2011). More recently, anthropology, with its insistence on highlighting actors' meanings and its ethnographic commitment to cultural variation, has taken seriously the idea that children are social agents. There are a number of relevant themes. First, the emphasis on children's agency is evident in the way that anthropologists privilege the idea of children as meaning makers. Toren (2007) refers to the ways that children like adults are capable of reinterpreting long-held practices within families and communities. Three different sets of Fijian children at different points in time were asked to reflect and draw pictures of a Fijian domestic focal point, the Sunday Dinner. Toren's (2007) analysis of these drawings in the different time periods allowed her to discern subtle differences in the way that the Fijian children viewed this ritual over time and were thus able to impute meaning to long-held cultural practices.

Secondly, anthropology promotes children's agency in the way that it challenges developmental theory. Bluebond-Langner (1994) argues that children are able to impute meaning to conventional taboo subjects such as death. She argues that this is particularly poignant and significant for children living with life-shortening diseases. Here anthropologists adopt an ethnographic approach, allowing them to get close to the respondents' lifeworlds. Sometimes this means that children conform to developmental expectations of ages and stages of cognitive growth in the way that they understand death in terms of 'childish' fantasies. At other times the same children have a much more mature and insightful understanding of their conditions due to the long-term process of children living with their illnesses and becoming aware of the implications of their conditions. Children here impute meaning to their lives way beyond the expectations of adult professionals with responsibility for their medical care. This has implications for the children and carers, with the former more likely to be involved in decisions affecting their care (Alderson 1994).

Thirdly, anthropological research on children and childhood as with research in other disciplines has challenged the idea of a unitary model of childhood based on the child as a social incompetent. As Montgomery (2008, p. 1) argues, anthropologists 'have shown consistently that the idea of a universal child is an impossible fiction and that children's lives are influenced as strongly by their culture as by their biology'. Children in a range of disparate contexts belie their biological inferiority in the way that they routinely contribute to their families and communities through the work that they undertake within the home and in terms of work they do outside the home that sometimes helps to sustain the material wellbeing of families and communities. Berman (2011), in her ethnography of K'iche' children from Guatemala, explores a different role that children play in mediating between adults from different families. Children run errands, convey messages and provide an important buffer between groups of disputing adults. Children play this important mediate role ironically because they are not seen as significant players within their communities and less likely to upset different families and groups of adults in dispute. Children's agency here emerges from a complex and often conflictual set of relationships within communities.

Fourthly, children are characterized by some anthropologists as being both vulnerable and agentic (Bluebond-Langner and Korbin 2007). Within a broader structural context children's agency challenges and complicates their hitherto status as vulnerable human 'becomings'. A critical role for anthropologists is to tease out the relationship between these two features of childhood within localized contexts. Fifthly, an anthropology of childhood is also influenced by a more powerful global political agenda on childhood. Rosen (2007), for example, refers to the 'straight 18' position of many global humanitarian organizations. In the pursuit of child protection, policy agendas often draw a clear boundary between those under the age of eighteen, children and those eighteen and over, adults. Rosen's particular focus is the recruitment of those under the age of eighteen for military service and the proscription of those child soldiers for war crimes. The logic of agency here is that an anthropological sensibility identifies the different ways that children exercise their agency as child soldiers. It also makes it difficult for children to be redefined as vulnerable where legal action could be taken against children for alleged war crimes.

Children's geographies

Children's agency has been associated with the concept of children's spaces within the developing field of children's geographies. Geographers have been concerned here to locate agency and space within a broad range of areas and themes ranging from the implications of transnational migration for children through to transport policy and children's involvement in the micro politics of families (Pratt 2010; Barker 2003). One key question posed by children's geographers is: 'how do children who live in certain urban environments develop their agency?' (Zeiher 2003, p. 68). With a perceived increase in the regulation of children, particularly in more affluent urban settings, geographers here identify a range of everyday life strategies adopted by children in taking some control of what Zeiher (2003) calls 'children's individual life spaces'. As with the other disciplinary approaches discussed earlier in the chapter, agency is embedded in children's daily lives. Agency here is about children shaping their routines and in turn helping to construct a variety of environmental factors that impinge on their lives. There is the working through of Giddens' (1984) notion of structuration here. Thus children are able to have some control over decision-making processes such that they are altered and become a routinized part of future norms and regulations. One example is the way that two German boys from different social class backgrounds are able to negotiate the 'temporal structure of their afternoons', that is, they are able in different ways to have some control over how they spend their free time after school (Zeiher 2003, p. 74).

While geography and use of physical space dominates analyses of common and diverse features of children's lives, there is also considerable emphasis placed on the social class dimensions of children and childhood. Thus Zeiher (2003) refers to the different ways that working-class and middle-class children in a German city manage their free time once they get home from school. There are some interesting class differences: Daniel, a 10-year-old working-class boy, has to make decisions about how to spend his free time with respect to the kind of access he has to a group of friends and peers. Thomas, a 10-year-old middle-class boy, on the other hand, tends to negotiate his peers on a more independent basis, with individual friendships being more significant than group affiliations. In many respects the spatial location of their respective families shapes the way these boys are able to exercise any agency. Daniel's family lives much closer to a range of locations or 'islands' where he is able to spend his free time with his friends and where his parents have fewer concerns about the time he plays with his friends away from the home. As his leisure time can be spent locally, his decisions about how and with whom to spend this time are 'tied to the moment', there is little forward planning needed (Zeiher 2003, p. 71). Thomas and his family live in a middle-class district of the city much further away than these 'islands', which include the city park and a swimming pool. He needs to know in advance which of his friends are available and when they can accompany him to the park or the swimming pool. He also needs to negotiate with his parents, or the parents of his friends, access to these places as he relies on them for getting across the city. The exercise of agency in terms of shaping his free time is less spontaneous involving more planning. For Daniel the local streets are a site for recreation with easy access between home and play. For Thomas, on the other hand, the streets are a means to gaining access to more distant recreational sites.

Children's conceptions of agency

So far I have concentrated on a range of different disciplinary approaches to children's agency. The focus here has been on the vantage points of *adult* researchers. In this final part of the chapter I want to examine the conceptions that children themselves have of their agency. In general terms, research since the mid-1990s has documented the importance children attach to agency in an implicit sense in the way that children constantly refer to their lack of voice or 'not having a say'. There is only a limited body of work on how children understand the concept of their agency. There is, however, rather more research on children's participation than there is on agency here. Nevertheless, as I have argued earlier, the two concepts are closely related, with participation presupposing levels of agency. Moreover, children's assessment of voice or participation acts as a proxy for a lack of agency in their lives (personal communication Pia Christensen). As has been well established in childhood studies, hitherto, children have tended to argue that they have limited access to communication channels and negligible influence over most decisions directly affecting them and their families.

When children reflect on the concept of voice within research and professional contexts, three themes are prominent and inter-related: participation is an entitlement rather than a gift; participation has to be based on identifiable outcomes that improve their school experiences and their recognition as agents in school and the success of initiatives that promote their agency emerge from ongoing relations with school staff. First of all there is an important social justice component to children's agency; children argue that they should not be discriminated against simply in terms of age (Hill 2006; Stafford et al. 2003). This conceptualization of agency comes out of the United Nations Convention on the Rights of the Child (CRC) in that rights are about the establishing of children's human capacities. While there is recognition of differences between children and adults – the preamble to the Convention states that children should be given 'special care and assistance' – they are still entitled to the same respect and dignity to which adults are entitled – children are ontologically fixed as 'human beings' (UN 1989). While the Convention emphasizes the need to provide for and protect children, in its insistence that children have an identity and a culture the Convention also establishes children as full social members with a right to be respected.

In an earlier survey of children's views on voice, a sample of Scottish children argued that they wanted to be consulted on a number of key issues, among them, the content of their learning; the social conditions of their schools; issues relating to health education and access to leisure facilities (Stafford et al. 2003). This was based on the teaching staff recognizing their agency through an acceptance of citizenship type status within the school and the classroom. Moreover, this consultation had to involve all children in their schools based on the principles of fairness and equity rather than children being selected by the teaching staff. From my own research with school councillors in England, there is a commitment from the councillors to gaining some recognition from school staff and a willingness to demonstrate how capable they are in contributing to the common good of the school. There is a complex relationship between the children in the school and the teaching staff. There are mixed views on the presence of teachers in school council meetings. While some viewed the meetings as an autonomous space within which school-related issues could be discussed away from teacher surveillance, others saw the presence of teachers as a way of demonstrating their capacities; as a evidence that teachers were committed to working with them and as a strategy for ensuring the younger members of school councils had their voices taken seriously (Wyness 2003). There was also an explicit social dimension to children's agency. While there was a tendency among some teaching staff to concentrate on pupil voice as a mechanism for gaining greater legitimacy of school policy on the curriculum and behavioural policy, the councillors saw their roles partly to improve the collective social wellbeing of children in the school including improving social spaces such as playgrounds and lunch halls. Children here were trying to expand or at the very least consolidate what little social space they had left in the school (Fielding 2006).

School councils are one important way for adults and children to discuss relevant issues. More generally adult–child consultations, which in the past have come in for a lot of criticism for their lack of authenticity, are often viewed by children as one way of children exercising agency (Thomas 2007). Timely consultations with adults are often preferable to adult-free contexts where children have to weigh up their commitment to participatory forums against a desire to retain control over their 'free' time (Hill 2006). Thus adult-free participatory initiatives are generally seen as more time con-suming in terms of their development and maintenance. Given that this often means children having to give up their own time within or out-of-school time this can have a knock-on effect on children's own leisure time.

While there is a strong message from children that voice and agency are signalled as respect as human beings, there also has to be a purpose to the dialogue between children and school staff: consultations have to be oriented to specific changes in their school experiences. In other words, children's voices have to carry weight, there have to be appreciable outcomes to any consultation. Children take a pragmatic line here balancing commitments to school voice with school work, home life and peers. Importantly then as well as seeing agency as an end, children are also outcomes oriented: having a voice is viewed as a means to generating change (Hill 2006). Children make a number of pragmatic judgements when it comes to assessments about their capacities. They emphasize the relational dimension of voice and agency. Voice has to work and it can only do so if there is a receptive audience. Children are not searching for autonomy – although they do desire spaces away from the surveilling adults when reflecting on their interests and articulating them with their friends or peers. However, in general children stress the importance of working with adults. In a more global context there is some variation in the relationship that adults have with children in participatory contexts. Kranzl-Nagl and Zartler's (2010) study of participation across six European countries identified children's commitment to adults playing a facilitative rather than interventionist role in their participation. In Mason and Bolzan's (2010) cross-cultural research with children in the Asia-Pacific region, there was variation in the meaning of participation across the region. Nevertheless, one convergent claim made by the children was that participation involved working alongside adults. The emphasis on 'purposeful' modes of participation in school is the heightening of the relational dimension to their agency, they exercise agency in and through ongoing relations with their teachers. There is much less concern expressed about whether adults should be involved, and more emphasis placed on children's having some input into the type of method adopted by the researcher or the adult facilitator. Thus the issue here is not so much giving children more autonomy from adults within which they can participate, but creating an environment within which children feel more comfortable participating alongside adults.

In many ways the emphasis on children's agency and participation reflects changes that have taken place in the nature of adult–child relations and the way that childhood is conceptualized. This is discussed in more detail in the following chapter. What is worth noting here is that agency is paradoxical when discussing possible scenarios that develop out of the recognition of children's agency, particularly adults' awareness and acceptance of children's agency. In one sense the idea that children's agency implies degrees of autonomy and relative freedom from adults is sometimes challenged by children themselves. The clearest example of children's autonomy is to grant them a position within society that is at odds with the social conventions, and thus distances them from the protective and structured environments controlled by 'responsible' adults. As we saw earlier in the chapter the notion of the political child is sometimes seen as oxymoronic: children simply cannot inhabit political spaces. To talk of a political child is to remove children from their normal social contexts where they are less protected, less nurtured, in effect, more adult-like. While I discussed a number of historical and contemporary examples of political children which belie the claims made by Arendt, the point I want to make here is that children's political voices are sometimes at their most potent when they are calling for the return of adult authority potentially putting them in conflict with adults (Bethke Elshtain 1996).

There is a potentially paradoxical situation here: crudely speaking we give children the space within which to articulate their interests, which opens up the possibility for these interests to include the return of some form of adult authority, which would potentially weaken children's voices. One interesting example of this is the role that children and young people played in the anti-apartheid movement in South Africa in the 1960s and 1970s. While the main focus of the political activities of South African youth was the challenge to white minority rule, there was also a commitment to restoring 'normal' adult–child relations, in effect the attempted restoration of adult authority (Ndebele 1995). The perception among the young was the loss of adult leadership and guidance in the home and in the classroom. Ndebele talked about an 'ontological crisis' for black South African parents for both failing to bring about political change and being 'dismissed by children for having failed to protect them' (Ndebele 1995, p. 331). Children's commitment was not about increasing their power over adults or the creation of adult-free spaces for children, but a call for adults to give children more support and guidance, to re-establish their authority where children's voices are an integral part of 'normal' adult–child relations. This is an apparent paradox: children are in a position to call for radical social changes but this can only take place with adults. Moreover, children are asking adults to take more control, in a sense, to reclaim their authority but not in terms of a return to an earlier and arguably mythical authoritarian past, but through the introduction of more open dialogic and negotiable relations between adults and children.

What these children are calling for here is to have a voice and the respect from adults that goes with voice but not necessarily all the concomitant responsibilities that go with having a say, which are sometimes assumed when children are granted rights. This is more apparent when examining research on children and divorce. Birnbaum and Saini (2013) at a global level identify a variation in the proportions of children wanting to be involved in decisions relating to their parents' divorce. On occasion children whose parents are separating or getting divorced are telling us that they do not want to be burdened by the responsibility of having to take some part in decision making where there are crucial consequences for themselves or their families (Oswell 2013). In principle children now have more say when their parents are separating or getting divorced (children's legal agency is discussed in Chapter 2). Children's involvement in decision-making processes can often revolve around being informed and consulted about what is happening to them and their families. Children want to know that they matter or that they count when going through the divorce process with their parents, with children being listened to and recognized as important actors in this process (Maes, de Mol and Buysse 2011). Agency here is more about how parents and others can help children to find a role that 'allows (them) not only to speak but also to stay silent, to have some control...over the conditions of communication' (Oswell 2013, p. 106). Having agency here is not simply about participation or involvement it can entail children being in a position to choose to stand back and let adults take on the primary decision-making roles.

Conclusion

In this chapter I discussed children's agency from a range of different disciplinary vantage points and at a number of different levels of analysis. Historical analyses now include children as historical agents living through a number of significant events and periods. Anthropologists of children and childhood draw on agency in terms of childhood diversity. A more intensive and ethnographic research focus reveals a range of agentic roles that children play in a number of diverse social, political and geographic contexts. If we turn to geography, I have focused on the way that children routinely have some control over their use of time and space, despite a heightened increase of public concern and subsequent great regulation of children's lives. The emphasis here is on agency as a routine and hitherto unexamined feature of children's lives. In all three disciplines agency is conceptualized as a social, moral and embodied aspect of children's lives. The starting point for the analysis in this chapter is a sociological analysis of children's agency which favours these features rather than viewing agency as a relatively adult-free sphere of autonomy within which children's interests can be authentically articulated. In the final part of the chapter I explored the views of children themselves which reinforced the relational approach agency. There was also an undeniable commitment from children to working with adults in retaining and strengthening agency. Issues of respect and integrity were also central to their conception of agency as were the balanced emphases on justice and efficacy. Agency here was seen to be both a starting point and means to achieving certain ends as well as an end in itself (Prout 2000).

2
The Recognition and Distribution of Children's Agency

In the previous chapter I argued that there has been a shift of focus within the social sciences towards greater recognition of children as social agents. In this chapter we explore the significance of children's agency in broader social and political terms. In particular, I examine the extent to which this shift in focus can be found within public and private institutions where change has been a dominant theme. Is it possible to identify children's agency within broader patterns of political and social change? In the first section I focus on childhood itself, in particular a powerful public narrative that emphasizes the idea that contemporary childhood is in crisis. Drawing on public commentary at national and global levels, I discuss the terms of this debate and the extent to which this 'crisis' thesis is able to incorporate a conception of childhood agency. In illustrating the relationship between 'childhood in crisis' and the concept of agency, I focus on a key theme within the public realm, the 'premature sexualization' of children. The second part examines the political and policy dimensions of the public realm where children have now become more visible recipients of welfare and state support. To what extent does children's entitlement to welfare shift the way we conceptualize children's status as social agents? Does this shift in political status challenge the position of children within the family? In addressing these questions I focus on the changing nature of relations between the child, the family and the state. In the third section the emphasis shifts to family in more substantive terms with an analysis of children's agency merging from the changing nature of family relations. Family is often associated with ideas of privacy and intimacy, making it difficult for any change to children's status within the family to gain full public recognition. Nevertheless, I will refer to recent research which has focused on the changing nature of family and the potential this offers for renegotiating children's agency.

In the final section of the chapter I pick up on Fraser's (2000) imperative to reintroduce the language of inequality and redistribution. Parts 1 to 3 can be viewed in terms of both the limited recognition and misrecognition of children's agency. The emphasis here is on the public, institutional and privately defined status of children. There is a shift in the status of children that has received some degree of public recognition. Moreover, the major thrust within childhood studies has been to render visible the nature of children's agency. While asserting in more general terms children's status as social agents throughout the book, in this chapter I also want to focus on how this status materializes within different groups of children. Drawing on social class and age as two dimensions of difference, I will explore the different ways that children exercise their agency. In effect, I want to focus on the distribution of agency across the child population.

Children's agency and the crisis of childhood

I want to argue in this chapter that children's agency is a potent response to a range of public commentaries and analyses that implicitly or explicitly assert that childhood is in crisis (Wyness 1999; Buckingham 2000; Palmer 2006). However, the starting point for the analysis here is the absence of any understanding of children's capacities as social agents. Features of a modernist twentieth-century conception of childhood such as innocence and dependence are said to be compromised by high divorce rates, commercial pressures on children and an alleged rise in the number of children with mental health problems (Layard and Dunn 2009). The issues here partly revolve around the shifting roles and responsibilities of adults that allegedly compromise the relationship they have with children, exposing the latter to a range of 'postmodern' risks before they are developmentally ready. Rather than viewing adult–child relations more positively in terms of change and thus opening up the potential to view the child as more agentic, one side of the inter-generational relationship is argued to be in terminal decline.[1] In effect, this is a public narrative on social disorder, with children out of place, allegedly occupying 'adult' positions and thus challenging a 'natural' biologically driven generational order. In effect, agency is associated with deviance both in terms of the categorizing of childhood and in relation to how children's reactions to these pressures on themselves and their families are likely to be interpreted.

Premature sexualization

One key aspect of this alleged decline or disappearance of childhood is the way that public and private realms are argued to be suffused with sexual images and representations which children are confronted with now on a daily basis. Public commentary has referred to the 'premature sexualization' of children, where a quintessential feature of childhood, children's innocence, is eroded as children at an increasingly younger age are incorporated within an ever-expanding sexual discourse (Buckingham and Bragg 2004, p. 1). This alleged problem has global ramifications linked to what Fleer, Hedegaard and Tudge (2009, p. 5) call the 'corporatization' of childhood; childhood has been reconstructed in marketing terms with children aggressively targeted as consumers. In the UK, sectors of the press continually refer to the destruction of childhood in terms of young children being 'bombarded on all sides by pre-teen makeup, clinging clothes and magazines encouraging them to be Lolitas' (*The Daily Mail*, 24 July 2002, cited in Buckingham and Bragg 2004, p. 2), while *The Times Educational Supplement*, a respected educational broadsheet, reports on the 'chilling reading' and 'shocking' statistics claiming that around a quarter of all children aged between thirteen and fifteen receive 'sexually explicit' text messages or 'sexting' and 10% of 10 to 12-year-olds and 25% of 13 to 15-year-olds claim they have seen sexually explicit images online ('War Against the Sexualisation of Childhood', *Times Educational Supplement*, 5 August 2011).[2] Girls are a particular focal point here, with *The Daily Telegraph* reporting 'The generation of "damaged" girls' (2 February 2007, cited in Kehily 2012, p. 1).

A leading UK children's charity, the NSPCC, published a report entitled *Premature Sexualisation: Understanding the Risks* (2011) and makes explicit reference to the current UK government's commitment to tackling the problem. The latter was involved in commissioning the Bailey Review (DfE 2011) which responded to perceived pressures from parents that children need more protection from the 'sexualized wallpaper' that surrounds them.[3] The author Reg Bailey, the chief executive of the influential Mothers' Union, conflates 'sexualization' with 'commercialization', in asserting that parents should have a much stronger voice in regulating the roles that the media and big business play in connecting with the interests of children.

An Australian report on sexualization with the more provocative title 'corporate paedophilia' analyses girls' magazines, television programmes and advertising. The authors argue that the representation of young girls, particularly those under the age of twelve, is sexual, with children 'being dressed in clothing and posed in ways designed to draw attention to adult sexual features that the children do not yet possess' (Rush and La Nauze 2006, p. vii). In Norway the government has taken this a stage further by urging retailers to withdraw sexually provocative clothing for young girls (Rysst 2010). In the USA this concern has been picked up across a range of public and professional bodies (Cook and Kaiser 2004). The American Psychological Association, for example, has a particular focus on sexualized toys, such as Bratz dolls, being dressed in sexually provocative clothing, allegedly giving off the wrong signals to young girls (2007). Later, Bragg (2012) reported sexualization as a key public theme in a number of countries across Europe including Holland and France.

While the term 'sexualization' is poorly defined, it is generally taken to denote 'the imposition of adult sexuality on children and young people before they are capable of dealing with it' (Department for Education, cited in Bragg 2012, p. 408). These global concerns thus exemplify a dominant adult gaze that emphasizes notions of innocence and emotional and cognitive immaturity. Within these terms children are in a vulnerable position, easily influenced and corrupted, with limited capacities to resist the alleged ubiquity of these messages. This is a powerful public and global discourse with little or no acknowledgement that children themselves may have particular conceptions of sexualization and thus little sense that children are able to understand this 'sexualized wallpaper' in different terms. This dominant sexualized vantage point becomes far more complex if we refer to Rysst's (2010) work with 10-year-old Norwegian girls. Agency is a more prominent feature of her analysis, with girls being given the time and space to provide a counter narrative to sexualization. While the girls challenge their 'childish' status, the issue of their clothing and their general appearance revolves around wanting to look cool 'kul' and fashionable rather than 'sexy' in relation to their peers.

Buckingham and Bragg's (2004) interview and diary data from 120 children aged between nine and seventeen identify a number of key themes that at the very least complicate the pervasive message of 'premature sexualization'. Among other things the youngsters discerned conflicting messages about children's relationship to sex. There was an awareness of 'sexual' material in both adult and youth media which sometimes extolled the pleasurable aspects of sex but often referred to the dangers of sexual experimentation at too young an age. In effect, the youngsters were aware of the 'premature sexualization' agenda, often seeing this as a crude attempt to teach a moral code. They were resistant to the latter, favouring more subtle narratives often found in dramas and soap operas that gave them the space to come to their own judgements about sex and sexuality. Similarly, Kehily's (2012) ethnography of a group of English primary school girls focuses on the way that the girls draw on a range of sexual imagery from the media in playground games and discourse. The girls use this imagery to create fantasy games and role play within the relatively safe confines of the female peer group.

Girls have usually been the particular focus of the moral entrepreneurs' critique of sexualization, allegedly more at risk than boys and subject to forms of 'hypersexualization' (Bragg 2012). But just as Buckingham and Bragg's sample of children were critical of judgements being made about them by adult authorities, Pilcher's (2010) sample of young English girls aged between six and eleven reflected on the implications that fashion has for their own developing identities. While there were attempts to try on 'grown-up' clothing, there was also some awareness of 'the contradictions of femininity in contemporary culture' (Pilcher 2010, p. 469). The girls were both aware of the power of more sexually provocative clothing and the moral disapproval from others that this can generate. At the same time there was also a sense that 'dressing up' was a way of playing around with adult culture within the relatively regulated context of the home. Kehily (2012) also argues that this provides a relatively safe context within which children are able to develop their awareness of sexuality. What we are moving towards in this analysis is a more interpretive approach. That is, children have the capacity to ascribe meaning to allegedly 'adult' material in more complex nuanced ways. It is not simply a case of children internalizing sexual images and discourse as a unilineal process, a process that has a corrupting influence on their development. Buckingham and Bragg's (2004) research, in particular, gave their young respondents a platform from which they could respond to the dominant adult gaze on children and the sexual world. From a different vantage point, then, which takes account of children's perspectives, children's agency in the form of interpretation softens, if not challenges, the crisis thesis.

Family, state and children's agency

While there is some public ambiguity over the contemporary status of childhood, there has been some recognition of children's agency in the public domain of child-related policy and practice. However, in many Western liberal democracies and for much of the twentieth century children were legally and politically included within the family as dependants with parents representing their interests (Lewis 2006). In many of these countries a bipartite relationship developed between family and state: in the UK there has been an uneasy tension between the partial and particular interests of parents, and the state professionals with general interests in the wellbeing of children as investments in the future. Dingwall et al. (1995, p. 220) clearly set out this ambiguity in their ethnographic study of encounters between social workers and parents.

> They [the social services] cannot be given the legal power to underwrite an investigative form of surveillance without destroying the liberal family. At the same time, the state cannot opt out. There is a collective interest in the moral and physical wellbeing of future citizens, in the quality of social reproduction...

Moreover, the family, particularly in Western English-speaking countries, was viewed as the private realm, a repository of human values set against the external world within which the state plays a powerful interventionist role (West et al. 2009; Fahey 1995). Culturally, the family was seen as a retreat, haven or sanctuary vis-à-vis an interventionist political establishment (Mount 1982; Lasch 1977). Within a more global context, family acts as a bulwark against a politically oppressive state. Take, for example, the case of the former East Germany (GDR) where family in some cases was the only effective political opposition to the Soviet state (Du Bois-Reymond et al. 1993). Legal scholars have also referred to a culture of privacy in the USA, where the private is conflated with the family and the concept of home as the sphere of individual liberty in and against infringements to privacy from the state (Whitman 2004). The private family epitomized the conventional nuclear family with children hidden within its protective structures as dependants.

In political and policy terms agency was attributed to parents or professionals with children's agency largely unrecognized. Towards the end of the twentieth century there has been a significant legal shift in the focus from family to child, with the welfare of the child rather than integrity of family the state's priority. This shift in focus towards the child's welfare has led to the child being disaggregated or separated from parents in legal and political terms. Children are now more visible entities, making it more difficult to talk in terms of the perspective of 'the family'. The child as a separate entity is also a human-rights bearing individual and cannot any longer be so easily subsumed within the family as a 'dependant'.

This is articulated through a number of policies globally, including the Care of the Child Act (2004) in New Zealand, the 1992 Child Protection Act in Norway and the 1989 Children Act in England and Wales (Goldson 2006; Arild Vis and Thomas 2009). In the latter case this was clearly codified through the 'paramountcy' principle whereby the welfare of the child is the paramount concern of various agencies and professionals (Wyness 1999). In some respects children's agency has an uncertain position within these new political and legal arrangements. One key feature of political language over the past two decades, particularly in England and Wales, is the reference to 'parental responsibility'. Children's 'separate' status means that parents are less likely to be recognized as having proprietorial relations with their children. As there is a stronger emphasis on the individual child, social policy focuses on the parent as the responsible agent ensuring that children follow appropriate moral and social trajectories. Some parents, those experiencing difficulties with agencies, are more likely to interpret the emphasis on parental responsibilities as an implicit threat from outside. Family–state relations have a much more overtly hierarchical character here, with various state agencies having legal and social powers over families, and parents being delegated special rights and responsibilities for the care and protection of their children. Donzelot (1977) argues that in the nineteenth century it was politically and economically expedient for the modern nuclear family to take full responsibility for children's development and welfare. In the case of poorer working-class families these responsibilities were heavily circumscribed by welfare professionals. The concept of the responsible parent has been used in child protection and care, education and criminal justice realms to 'police' and sometimes punish poor disadvantaged parents. The issue of truancy is periodically covered by the media in the USA and UK with parents being targeted for their inability to ensure their children attend school ('More parents jailed as truancy rates soar', *Guardian*, 12 February 2009; 'Parents serve jail time with children for truancy', *News Channel 25*, 27 May 2010). Within a criminal justice context parents are subject to a range of orders as a consequence of their children's criminal activities, including being 'bound over to take proper care and exercise proper control over the child' (Hollingworth 2007, p. 193).

At the same time policy has focused on the role that children themselves play in their own welfare. In England and Wales the 1989 Children Act refers to the way that professionals working with children have to 'ascertain their wishes and feelings', thus emphasizing the voice that children have in a range of arrangements that were hitherto made by parents and professionals (Wyness 1999). Similarly, the 1995 Children Act in Scotland strengthened the well-established children's hearing panels in emphasizing the importance of adult members of panels consulting children (Arild Vis and Thomas 2009). At an international legal level this principle has been reinforced by the UN Convention on the Rights of the Child (CRC), where children have become more independent rights bearers. Articles 12 and 13 of the Convention introduce a more discursive dimension to children's wellbeing: children have 'voice'-based rights that in theory give them opportunities to articulate their interests in a number of different ways. There is some debate as to whether these rights are global and universal in scale or simply reflect the values of more Western affluent nation-states including individualism and self-reliance (Stephens 1995; Boyden 1997). I will develop this theme in more detail in Chapters 3 and 4. Nevertheless, it is generally accepted that the CRC provides the moral and political impetus to governments in promoting ways in which children can have a voice in arrangements that affect them.

Children's status as agents thus at some levels locates them outside of the family, particularly in relation to the ongoing relations between agencies of the state and the family. Rather than assuming a bipartite relationship between family and state, the child can be viewed as a more independent third party, generating a more complex tripartite or 'triangular' relationship between the interests of the state, parents and

children (Parton 2006). The influence of feminism is pertinent here: in the 1970s the position of women was propelled
into the public domain identifying hitherto less politically
visible members of the population as more agentic. The family
as an undifferentiated entity was challenged during this period
by feminism focusing on how the family as a private realm
oppresses and disadvantages women (Delphy 1984). The
family as the private realm makes it more difficult for the
domestic and child-related work carried out by women to be
recognized along the same lines as their male counterparts'
work within the workplace. Feminists were also active in
bringing issues of male power within the home into the public
domain; issues that were hitherto viewed as private domestic
issues. Domestic violence and latterly child abuse were recognized as public and political problems that demanded a
response from professionals and policy makers across the
public sector. The invisible status of women within the home
became a focal point with the position of women being re-
evaluated and individualized in terms of spaces for women
(Munro and Madigan 1993). This framework has later been
expanded to incorporate the position and status of children
within the family (Mayall 2002). The third-party status of
children further compromises and complicates assumed relations within family, thus reinforcing the contested nature of
family. The opening up of family to demands from women,
children and those working on behalf of the latter has generated considerable debate about the role that children now
play. One possibility here is the mediate role they play between
family and state.

These new political trends have created relatively new positions for children in and through negotiations and discussions
that they have with parents and professionals. While politically and legally there has been a shift towards separating and
individualizing children, in social and professional terms this
has usually been interpreted as a greater recognition of children. Children have an ontology within the family that in
some instances means generating more democratic relations
between the generations (Beck and Beck-Gernsheim 1995).
Child care and protection policy in England and Wales
through the 1989 and 2004 Children Acts emphasizes the
importance of consulting with children in matters relating to

their welfare. Research in England and Norway has suggested that these new roles for children are limited in that adult and professional agendas still dominate proceedings involving children and professionals (Arild Vis and Thomas 2009). Within a social work context, children themselves make the distinction between being consulted and taking an active role in decision making with greater involvement in the former than the latter (Holland et al. 2005). Children also appear to lack trust in professionals and state bodies and are reticent to call on them for help when they have difficulties (Parton 2006). Despite these reservations, children's voices are now more likely to be heard in consultation with parents and professionals (Arild Vis and Thomas 2009; Holland et al. 2005).

One major issue confronting professionals is how to respect children's agency within the family where there is an increased risk of abuse, and where children's voices are likely to be muted. Professionals and researchers point to the difficulties of identifying children as separate entities within their families. In tackling this issue one approach used by professionals has been to try to increase the dialogue between children and their parents through family-group conferences. Dalrymple (2002) reports on a small-scale piece of research where adult advocates were used to represent children as third parties, where social workers set up group conferences with parents from families who came to the attention of the child protection system. The rationale here for adults speaking on behalf of children is that children can advise their advocates on how they want to be represented at the meetings; and social workers and parents have an independent adult who is in a position to relay children's views and feelings. The data from the children support the proxy voices of adult advocates. Dalrymple's (2002) data from the child clients emphasize the importance of the advocates as independent and knowledgeable adults, able to advise less experienced children on the way the child protection system works in a confidential manner.

An alternative approach is to have the children physically present at these conferences. In Holland et al.'s (2005) research, professionals used these family-group conferences as open forums within which children, parents and social workers talk through a range of issues and problems. While the agenda-setting powers of the state and the social worker as 'expert' perspective were both evident, the authors note the attempts of the social workers to promote children's participation within these forums, particularly children who hitherto had little sense of voice within their families. Children were in a position to exercise some agency in the way that they talked about their feelings and requested more input into domestic decision-making processes between them and their parents.

Within an educational context a bipartite rather than tripartite relationship between family and state was clearly evident in policy in the late twentieth century. Education reform in English-speaking countries was trying to shift the balance of power away from educational professionals and local educational authorities towards educational 'consumers' with parents rather than children identified as the latter (Wyness 1999). The bipartite parent–school relationship is still a dominant feature of education policy in the USA (US Dept of Education 2010). For example, the Obama administration is committed to making education more of a parental responsibility. 'To parents, we can't tell our kids to do well in school and then fail to support them when they get home. You can't just contract out parenting. For our kids to excel, we have to accept our responsibility to help them learn' (Barack Obama, cited in US Dept of Education 2010). There is very little US educational policy material that refers to the involvement of children as partners or educational participants.

In the UK, on the other hand, there is some evidence from institutional practice in English and Welsh schools that children are starting to be incorporated as third parties. For example, the notion of a partnership or a more contractual relationship between home and school has created space for children to participate. Research on home–school relations picks up on the complexity of this tripartite relationship. Written communication between home and school in relation to activities that take place in the classroom and more formal reports now encourage contributions from children as well as parents. There is little consensus between school staff and parents over the presence of children at meetings involving parents and staff. However, children can sometimes use face-to-face contact with parents and teachers as a way of strengthening their point of view and providing balance between any possible disagreements that parents and teachers might have (Beveridge 2004).

Family and agency

Mayall (2002) focuses on the significance of family as a site within which children's agency is embedded in the relationships that children have with parents, siblings and friends. Mayall (2002) argues that relations in school are more formal and distant, at least in secondary school, making it more difficult for children to be recognized as moral agents. Agency emerges from routine ongoing commitments and relations with others where emotional investments are made. These relations are more likely to be found in the home than the school. Moreover, agency has become more prominent as a consequence of the restructuring of family. Early work on the European family emphasizes subtle shifts in the nature of generational relations with children acquiring agency in terms of having more control over their activities inside and outside the family (Coleman and Hendry 1999; Jones and Wallace 1992; Ferchhoff 1990). Children view the home as the site where they are moral agents, as we argued in the last chapter, a critical feature of children's agency (Mayall 2002). There has been a shift here from a more authoritarian based relationship to more democratic modes of reflexivity, where there is more acceptance of children as participants by parents and more awareness by children of their agency or ability to reflect on their environment and identities.

Contemporary work continues on these themes with more conflict and negotiation between children and their parents and where children are more likely to 'challenge parental authority *through* negotiation' (Williams and Williams 2005, p. 319); this study focuses on the importance of technology in mediating this shift. To take one example: at one level parents are able to utilize their children's access to a mobile phone to have some control over the children's access to the public realm. While the mobile phone extended the time children spent outside the family, at the same time it was also a device that children used to renegotiate curfews set by parents. However, the mobile phone allowed children to negotiate the distance and length of time away from home. Teenage children were able to assuage parental fears about their safety outside the home by arguing that their parents could always get in touch with them using the mobile phone. As one 15-year-old girl commented, 'as long as I've got my mobile on me and she [mother] can get hold of me...as long as she knows where I am, she doesn't mind' (Williams and Williams 2005, p. 325). Agency here was about the different ways in which children could negotiate the control that parents had over their use of time and public space.

Despite global trends towards single-unit families, there is still considerable variation in the form that family takes (Cheal 2008). This variation has become marked in the past forty years in more affluent countries with significant differences in structure over time and across social space. In the USA the multi-generational family is becoming more popular. Around 12% of children live in these 'extended' family forms due to the impact of migration, economic recession and an ageing population (Pew Social Trends 2010). At the other end of the spectrum there has been a more longstanding increase in the number of children having routinely to negotiate different households as their parents separate and divorce. Just under a quarter of UK children have experience of parental separation and divorce (Social Trends 2010). Here we can see a move towards breaking the link between biological and social parenting, with lone-parent families, step families and gay families emerging out of adults and children making multiple transitions in the life course. Family structure has become more diverse and complicated, generating familial networks within which children are immersed. Arguably then, there is more opportunity for agency to be displayed.

Mayall's (2002) work, for example, refers to the different ways that children's moral agency emerges in her conversations with girls who are brought up in multi-family settings. The girls have to negotiate the birth of younger siblings whose fathers are different from theirs, where their mothers are struggling with ill-health and poverty, and where their fathers live apart from their mothers. Children's moral agency here is embedded and stretched across a range of family and household settings. The girls in Mayall's study are able to reflect on the different ways that they relate to their parents, siblings and friends in negotiating a range of quite diverse circumstances. One 12-year-old interviewee, Sandra, had a close relationship with her mother. In the absence of her father within the household, she spent a lot of time helping her mother to look after her younger siblings. Sandra reports on the birth of her youngest sibling and the difficulties that her mother experienced during the labour. Sandra was both knowledgeable about the process of giving birth and her mother's condition (having an emergency Caesarean due to pre-eclampsia). She was also able to think through the implications of her new sibling for her relationship with her mother and able to reflect more broadly on the implications of having another child within her family (Mayall 2002, pp. 90–4).

Divorce has become a recurring feature of family life since the late twentieth century. I referred in the last section to legislation in the UK that has emphasized the voices of children where they come into contact with professionals. This is the case for children at the centre of custodial battles between parents where legal professionals have a duty to consult with children. Yet, these consultations come towards the end of the divorce process. Children are clearly embedded in relations with parents at a much earlier stage of this process and it is here that children's agency is more likely to be demonstrated. Much has been written about the effects of divorce on children. Hitherto the emphasis has been on the negative consequences for children as victims of their parents' separation ('The cruelty of women who use children as weapons in divorce', *Daily Mail*, 22 September 2010). More recent research has focused on the different ways that children negotiate and come to terms with their parents' separation. In the post-divorce situation children were often prominent mediators when custodial arrangements were being made. If we look a little more closely at the kinds of deliberations made by children and separated parents, research from the UK and Norway on the roles that children play in post-divorce families identifies the way that children try to maintain equality between separate biological parents' households in terms of the amount of time they spend in each household (Haugen 2010; Neale and Flowerdew 2007). In the process of trying to maintain equity in terms of custodial arrangements, children play important mediating roles in maintaining the communication channels between the different households.

The concept of resilience has become a more prominent part of research on children living through difficult circumstances (McAdam-Crisp 2006). While it has tended to be used to describe the psychological wellbeing of the individual child, it has also been used to depict the capacities of children to manage divorce. Adjustments are made by children moving into lone-parent families. Hetherington (2003) in her research on US children and divorce argues that small groups of resilient children, children who are 'competent at a cost', take on too many responsibilities in the post-divorce situation. Children here are 'overburdened', particularly adolescent girls as they take on more adult type responsibilities in the absence of a father figure around the home (2003, p. 223). Children also adjust to new family forms as they move from a relatively stable lone-parent family situation to a step family. Step families have become a more common feature of children's social landscape in the UK with around 10% of all children now living in step families with many of these children likely to experience further disruptions as these new family formations break down (Flowerdew and Neale 2003). Nevertheless, the consistent rise over the past generation or so in the numbers of children having to move from a biological nuclear family to a lone-parent family and then into a step family certainly exercises children's capacities to manage new family situations sometimes with great rapidity. Children are able to negotiate multiple transitions which generate new family relationships throughout their childhoods as they move in and out of different family forms. The speed of change is significant: these changes are easier to cope with when the pace of change is relatively slow and where only one parent is re-partnering at a time. Girls are adept at helping to fill the gap when one parent, usually the father, moves out of the household.[4] Quite often girls take on more responsibilities within the home and find it difficult to adjust when their mother acquires a new partner and attempts are made to reconstitute the two-parent family. Despite these difficulties experienced by some children the move in and out of (and back into) the nuclear family is one that children are able to adapt to. As Flowerdew and Neale (2003, p. 151) comment on their sample of children from divorced families,

> [t]here is clear evidence in our study that with several years of post-divorce family life behind them, children's sense of what constitutes the 'complete' family has often shifted radically. What was an 'extraordinary' period of transition in their lives had become wholly 'ordinary'.

The social distribution of agency

While there is an ongoing debate over the recognition of children's agency, within a broader context of social and political change in Western societies, one key area that needs to be explored is the distribution of agency. In the first few parts of this chapter we located children and childhood within broader political and policy contexts of change and focused more generally on how children are affected by this change as social agents. In discussing the distribution of agency we will focus on issues of social inequality and two dimensions of difference. First of all, we examine children's social class status in terms of two themes, the institutionalization of agency and the mediation of poverty. Secondly, we focus on conceptions of children's agency as plotted along the life course in terms of chronological age. In other words, we examine the importance of agency with respect to differences between older and younger children.

Social class and the institutionalization of agency

The institutionalization of agency arises out of political and policy arrangements discussed earlier in the chapter that generate powerful expectations among child professionals as to the meaning of children's agency. Earlier in the chapter I touched on agency in terms of the third-party role of children. If children are disaggregated from families as independent rights bearers, what might the implications be for families from very different social, economic and cultural backgrounds? In referring back to Holland et al.'s (2005) work on family-group conferences there was a commitment among the professionals to hear children's voices along with those of their parents, and in many respects children reported being in a position to articulate their interests at these conferences. Holland et al. (2005) claim that family-group conferences had beneficial effects on family relations. Through follow-up interviews with participants six months later, children reported that they felt in a stronger position to have their say in family affairs. At the same time the conference agendas were heavily institutionalized, with professionals structuring the agendas and the discussions. While the professionals took account of the level of resources in each family, the demands made by professionals to continue the 'democratic' dialogue of the conference sometimes felt heavy handed. For example, in the conferences the social workers made lists of agreed areas and topics with the families and these were to be taken away by the families to be acted upon in their own private time.

There is also the suggestion that on occasion the 'voicing' of children may be at the cost of parents, which could potentially lead to more conflict within the families. Thus the creation of spaces for children's voices is interpreted by parents as a challenge to their sense of authority. We can only speculate here: the move towards more democratic relations where children have stronger voices is less likely to develop in poorer families. Here there is likely to be evidence of communication structures found within what Bernstein (1971) called 'position-oriented' families. The generational order is more hierarchical, with positions and roles relatively fixed; parents having more overt power and authority. There is limited discursive space to reason and negotiate between the generations: parents tend to assert their power and authority over their children through imperative commands and language that offer fewer opportunities for dialogue with children. This is contrasted with a more middle-class discursive model: the 'person-oriented' family, where there is more fluidity between the generations, personalities being as important as generational positions. Within the context of the former the distribution of agency across generations is probably limited; parents are more likely to view the promotion of children's voices as a form of intrusion. There are two possible sets of implications here. First, the distribution of agency exacerbates tensions that already exist within the family between parents and between parents and the children. Secondly, and more generally, there is a culture clash between middle-class professional values and the more traditional working-class values, with the former disrupting the latter. Parents view the relationship with the state in more negative hierarchical terms with children's agency viewed as another set of criteria against which they can be judged.

Lareau (2011) makes a similar distinction to Bernstein. In her ethnographic study of US 'lower' and middle-class families she distinguishes between the dynamics, language and atmosphere found in both family types. In middle-class families the emphasis is on children's social and intellectual development from a very early age. Children are viewed as the projects of parents in terms of what Lareau calls 'concerted cultivation'. Children grow up within a much more rational and verbal context. Here there is a much stronger sense of their entitlements among children to a voice and an opinion. Agency here is discursive and fluid with the home environment much more open to ideas. Lower or working-class families, on the other hand, are typified by the *'accomplishment of natural growth'*. Parents' child-care strategies here revolve around stressing children's emotional and social well-being with their intellectual growth being left more to fate or more concretely seen as the responsibility of the school teacher. There is much less dialogue and reasoning here and therefore fewer opportunities for children to display more legitimate discursive forms of agency (to be discussed in the following chapter). Lareau's (2011) conceptualization of class differences comes close to Evans' (2006) ethnographic study of working-class life in South London. Here the comparison is between the author's own 'concerted cultivation' approach to her own children's lives and the working-class mothers in her study. In the latter case parenting revolved around children's physical and emotional care. The emphasis on 'natural growth' was important here, with parents having little commitment to intervening in their children's lives in order to improve their life chances. A combination of material disadvantages and a belief that their children's intellectual growth was genetically pre-ordained rendered attempts at parental intervention both challenging and futile.

Lareau's work is influenced by Bourdieu and in particular the idea that the form of agency that is developed and encouraged within the middle-class home allows children to slot into school life without too many problems. Schools thus become an important means of social reproduction with middle-class parents ensuring their children's class positions are maintained if not enhanced through the connections they make with the schools and the teachers. There is as it were a more general expectation in schools in both state and private sectors in the more affluent world that parents are involved in the concerted cultivation of their children (Ball 2003). Working-class children and their parents have more difficulties adjusting to these expectations of what we might call the discursive child. In Bourdieu's terms working-class children lack the ability to generate cultural capital to connect with the dominant middle-class culture found within state schools (Bourdieu and Wacquant 1992). If we address agency and social class in terms of schooling and participatory initiatives directed at children rather than families, then we potentially have similar issues facing working-class children as opposed to middle-class children.

Drawing on the work of Bourdieu (Bourdieu and Wacquant 1992) there are issues around the child's ability to acquire social and cultural capital through school practices that heighten children's agency. In returning to participation in school, data from my own research in England suggest that children from poorer backgrounds are less likely to connect with participatory initiatives in school than their more affluent counterparts (Wyness 2009b). Secondary-school children involved in participatory initiatives both in school and outside of school within the local community were asked to assess the level, form and membership of their councils. With reference to the latter some councillors argued that schools tended to focus on confident, articulate and high achieving children who were likely to be involved in a range of initiatives in school, referred to by one councillor as the 'usual school child' (Wyness 2009b, p. 546).

These were children who were familiar with the school norms and structures and immersed in the culture of the school. Moreover, particular forms of participation in school, for example, membership of a school council, was seen by one respondent as an opportunity for more affluent children to display their agency. This in turn had a negative effect on the ability of less educationally able children to participate. As one adult coordinator of a city youth council commented: 'it's just another opportunity for young people's involvement has gone. It's being taken up by somebody who's already got an avenue to make their voice heard' (Wyness 2009b, p. 547). In these terms voice and by implication agency are class based. The claim here is that middle-class and academically oriented students tend to gravitate towards school councils, arguably those who are least likely to need political representation (Giroux 1989, p. 199). Children who were struggling with their schooling, in terms of learning or behaviour and those children intermittently outside of the school system, those excluded from schools, were likely to see attempts at introducing greater pupil voice in school as further alienating them from school. For these children the processes that precede the setting up of school councils and the election or selection of school councillors were likely to be viewed as obstacles to their involvement. This further reduced their capacity to participate and develop the cultural capital required to succeed within the school system.

White and Choudhury (2007) within an international development context make a similar claim in arguing that there is a tendency for participatory initiatives that heighten children's agency to be 'taken over' by middle-class children. They use the example of an Indian television programme which explored the lives of poor children. Despite the topic of poverty the programme makers included a sample of middle-class children. These children along with the more articulate poorer children were selected to present the programme. This selection was justified by the children themselves who claimed that they were more articulate than their poorer counterparts, better able to demonstrate the plight of working-class children in India than working-class children themselves.

Mediating poverty

Poverty has a major impact on excluding children in school and more broadly within society. Ridge (2006) refers to the ways that children talk about being excluded from 'normal' things including school trips, membership of clubs, access to leisure facilities and participation as consumers. Poverty also makes it difficult for children to participate with their peers in a range of leisure activities due to the prohibitive cost of these activities. Thus poverty can have an isolating experience with children in school bullied by their peers and made to feel different and inferior. In one sense then we can say that this has implications for children's agency if we associate agency with children's ability to participate. The general lack of resources and opportunities both to participate and to challenge obstacles to their participation restricts children's agency (Ridge 2006).

However, agency is also about children's capacity to make a difference to their circumstances and those around them. At another level children in poverty draw on their agency in mitigating a lack of social and political participation. Thus agency can also operate in the absence of participation. Children are able to mediate their poverty in a number of ways. First there are the demands made on families by schools which can lead to what Ridge calls children's 'self-denial of need' (Ridge 2006, p. 31). Children conceal the need to replace school uniforms by carefully hiding their old and worn uniforms from their parent. They are less likely to pass on requests to parents for resources needed from school. They are also less likely to tell parents that they are being bullied because of the way they look or quite simply due to their poverty. In effect, children are trying to protect parents from the guilt and embarrassment of being poor. Secondly, children take on part-time work in order to offer their parents some financial respite from the demands of consumerism (Leonard 2004). Thus the conventional view of children's part-time work providing them with non-essential money and having socializing functions is challenged in the way that children contribute to the domestic economy taking the pressure off parents to provide them with consumer goods that keep them in line with their peers.

Age and agency

One issue that has plagued advocates of children's agency, an issue that also has much broader importance within childhood studies, is the age at which children are said to be in a position to exercise agency. One way of tackling this issue is to place limits on the age at which children have a capacity for agency. Buckingham and Bragg (2004, p. 240) in researching childhood and sexuality discussed in the previous chapter argued that younger children have more difficulty interpreting references to sex within the media. Alderson (2008), on the other hand, argues that the issue of age and agency is much less relevant, with children almost from birth having a capacity for agency. She uses the example of infants 'shar(ing) in their own health care' in the way that they help their carers with feeding, eating and dressing (Alderson 2008, p. 29). The relational dimension to agency is prominent here with children able to exercise agency through and with their parents. One approach that assumes young children have agency and has influenced professional practice in early years' educational contexts is the Mosaic approach (Clarke and Moss 2001). Pre-school children are incorporated into research practice through a number of techniques that emphasize the role of the adult educator and carer as an observer of children's practices and a respecter of children's voices. Various research methods are adopted in engaging with preliterate children, including map making and photography which enable them to influence the agenda of the setting.

The relationship between agency and age is a feature of discussions on the methodological and ethical issues researchers encounter working with children. While agency is a taken for granted feature of researching children, there is still a tendency for researchers to take into account the age of the child respondent when selecting research methods. Much of the research discourse here has emphasized the child respondent as a co-constructor or collaborator, a more equal relationship between researcher and child (Christensen and James 2008). This reflects the assumption that children are social agents and competent enough to take a more active participatory role within the research process. Nevertheless, a number of research strategies and methodologies are generated to partly accommodate the age of the children being researched (Chakraborty 2009). Child researchers are now more likely to draw on a wider range of children when constructing a sample, with much younger children likely to be included. Nevertheless, there is still a tendency to leave data from younger children out of research reports and papers when using quotations from child respondents (Mantle et al. 2006). Much younger children are still deemed to be less competent in providing researchers with narratives of their lives and the lives of others.

At a policy and practice level, age is a significant differentiating factor when referring to agency. Professionals still tend to talk about whether a child is old enough to take part or contribute to decision-making processes. Children are still assessed against a Piagetian frame within which judgements are made according to ages and stages (Mantle et al. 2006). However, there are two trends that potentially refine and in some cases challenge these practices. First, Article 12 of the CRC is a significant reference point for professionals (discussed in more detail in the following chapter). While it emphasizes the importance of children's voice it also attaches a number of conditions to the operation of this voice. Among other things, judgements are made by adults as to the maturity as well as age of children before children are both capable of speaking and having that voice taken seriously. In theory then an assessment has to be made about levels of maturity that may not always coincide with age and age-related markers of competence. Second, at a practitioner level in the UK, these requirements have become an integral principle for those working with children through the invocation of 'Gillick competence' (Wheeler 2006). This concept developed from a 1985 legal case when a mother, Victoria Gillick, took her health authority to court because her 15-year-old daughter was prescribed contraception by her doctor without her consent. At the end of a lengthy legal process the UK Court appeal found in favour of the health authority on the basis of the following principle:

> …whether or not a child is capable of giving the necessary consent will depend on the child's maturity and understanding

and the nature of the consent required. The child must be capable of making a reasonable assessment of the advantages and disadvantages of the treatment proposed, so the consent, if given, can be properly and fairly described as true consent. (Children's Legal Centre 1985, p. 12)

There is no explicit reference made to age in this judgment. As with Article 12 of the CRC, medical practitioners and social workers assess whether a child is able to give the necessary consent to particular courses of action on the basis of levels of maturity.

Conclusion

In this chapter I have taken a broader political and institutional approach in assessing the significance of children's agency. Issues of recognition and misrecognition are important here. In the latter case public commentary on the changing nature of childhood obscures any conception of children having agency. There is recourse to a modernist risk-averse conception of childhood. This is particularly the case when examining the discourse on the sexualization of childhood, with a global consumer market a key protagonist and issues of innocence and protection at the forefront. Children's agency is at best seen as a distraction where demands are made to regulate the media and the global market. However, there is a degree of ambiguity, with children quite capable of reading the 'sexual wallpaper' in a number of non-threatening ways. My argument here is that children's agency rescues the concept of childhood in that by focusing on agency we can generate a different conception of childhood that fully immerses children in social institutions within a context of rapid social change.

We can see some elements of this change in our analysis of agency in relation to the broader political and policy domain. In this chapter I have looked at changes to the state and family both relationally and substantively. In the former case the political and policy realms have recast the state–family dichotomy as a more complex network of relations between parents, child professionals and children. The shift to a more tripartite arrangement offers the potential for children to play more formative roles in mediating between family and state. Changes that have taken place within families over the past generation or so have helped to expand and embed children's agency within their families. While these roles are still largely hidden within the borders of the family, researchers have started to acknowledge the different kinds of agency to emerge from routine child–parent interactions.

In the final part of the chapter, the focus switches from more general claims about children's agency to an analysis of how agency is distributed across the child population. While there is a degree of recognition of children's agency at a general political level, the diversity of childhood, the distinctive economic, social and political contexts within which children grow up, generate distinctive modes of agency. There are a number of social dimensions that differentiate the child population and in this chapter we focused on social class and age. In very crude terms social inequality as defined by socioeconomic and age-related criteria determines the quantity and quality of agency with which children are able to deploy. Two points are critical here: first, despite the difficulties that children might face due to their class and age positions, children are still capable of exercising their agency in the interests of themselves, their families and peers. Second, if agency is conceptualized in terms of participation then there are legitimate and socially sanctioned forms of children's agency, particularly found within schools in affluent societies. This framing of agency leads to the misrecognition of children's activities outside the frame. Children who struggle with the rules and norms of schools are not only likely to be socially excluded from the school system, they may openly reject the social and moral structures that underpin schools. These activities are less likely to be recognized in terms of children's agency. This brings us back to the problem of identifying children's agency within the discourse on sexualization. Are children's actions indicative of precocious and 'adultified' lifestyles or a reflection of changing social and cultural values that have incorporated children's agency? It is this tension between recognition and misrecognition that we turn to in the next two chapters when we explore the global context to childhood.

3
Childhood, Globalization and Global Standards

Much has been written about globalization: Scholte (2005, p. xvii) in his critical introduction argues that 'ideas on globalization have readily become so diverse, so broad, so loose, so changeable – in a word, so elusive – that one can pronounce virtually anything on the subject'. Thus, while the definition and conceptualization of globalization are broad what we can say is that a number of political, economic and cultural forces allied to major technological changes over the past thirty or forty years have enabled the quicker and more fluid movement of material goods, services, people and ideas across national borders. Mittelman (1997, p. 78) refers to this as '[t]he compression of time and space aspects of social relations, a phenomenon that allows the economy, politics and culture of one country to penetrate another'. In this chapter we will explore how these global processes or what Ongay (2010, p. 373) terms the 'macro flows of population, information and economics' affect children and our understandings of childhood. In the first part of the chapter we discuss the economic and political dimensions of globalization and their implications for children. One key feature of economic globalization is the intensification of migration both within and across borders. In order to exemplify the former and tease out the significance of globalization for children and their families,

I will look at the case of China and the mass movement of migrants from rural to urban regions. This is followed by a discussion of the political dimensions of globalization and the implications they have for children.

In the second part of the chapter the focus is on the global meaning of childhood. We go on to explore a dominant unitary model of childhood, a Western, affluent world view of childhood held up as a norm by international organizations and powerful nation-states. The emphasis here is on the political and cultural features of globalization. In particular, drawing on policy material from international organizations, we outline a postmodern conception of childhood as a global standard. I argue that in Western contexts an earlier 'modern' twentieth-century childhood has subtly changed to accommodate the rights agenda and a range of technological innovations that emphasize the agency of childhood. As I argued in Chapter 2 there is now a broad expectation among academics, practitioners and policy makers that children have access to an array of communication channels that strengthen their voices and their opportunities to participate. This is set against a range of childhoods found within less affluent regions of the world, conceived as deficit childhoods that need to be brought up to a global standard (Fleer, Hedegaard and Tudge 2009; Boyden and de Berry 2004).[1] We will discuss the relationship between this global standard and major global issues affecting children which generate these deficit models. One such problem is child labour. There has been considerable debate over the incidence, the prevention and the ending of child labour (Liebel 2007; ILO 2006). We will pick up on these themes in the following analysis. I want to illustrate the cultural and political implications of a global standard of childhood by referring to the child labourer as a globally deviant category of childhood. Drawing on international policy agendas on childhood, I will argue that an international commitment to ending child labour has led to a situation where the material work that children do does not count as a legitimate form of children's participation. In regions where child labour is recognized as a problem this has implications for how childhood is conceptualized.

Globalization and the impact on children

Economic globalization

There is some debate over the extent to which we are moving to a single global economy based on free market principles. Neo-liberals have argued that capitalism has globalized with labour, capital and finance moving with rapidity across a 'borderless' world (Ohmae 1990). Others have argued that the development of regional trading blocs and some dispersal of economic power to less affluent regions weaken any inevitable move towards a 'global economy' (Prout 2005; Yeung 1998). Nevertheless, the scale of trade between countries and regions has significantly changed, with multi-national corporations (MNC) now central economic players accounting for around three-quarters of all global trade and output (Hevener Kaufman et al. 2002). This has led to MNCs setting up production centres across the globe in regions with favourable economic conditions, with some nation-states lifting barriers to trade. There is thus a much greater movement of economic activity across national borders; what Katz refers to as the 'flexibility and spatial fluidity of capital' (2004, p. 179). This shift in scale and speed has generated some advantages with some countries' living standards having improved sufficiently. Among other things, this has led to children having greater access to health care and schooling and there has also been a significant reduction in the numbers of underweight infants (United Nations 2012). Globally, infant mortality rates have reduced from around 61 deaths per 1,000 live births in 1990 to 37 deaths per 1,000 live births in 2011 (WHO 2013).

However, there are major global and regional disparities. Economic globalization has not led to significant changes in the global distribution of income. There are still major inequalities when comparing the richest and poorest sectors of the global population. The top 20% of the global population enjoys 83% of income, whereas the bottom 20% has access to around 1% of the world's income. Moreover, these trends are exacerbated if we incorporate the distribution of wealth including financial assets and property into the analysis. Thus the Gini index, a recognized measure of economic inequality, is higher for wealth than income when assessing the distribution of economic inequality globally (Ortiz and Cummins 2011). Regionally things are more complex. Drawing on the Gini index for income distribution, the regions with the highest level of income including Europe, North America and countries from the Pacific Rim have the lowest level of inequality (30.9). Sub-Saharan Africa and Latin America are the regions with the highest levels of inequality (48.3 and 44.2 respectively). At the same time, of the six regions examined by Ortiz and Cummins (2011) only sub-Saharan Africa has become less unequal at the beginning of this century with income inequality widening in all other regions during this period. At a national level the fastest growing and largest economies in the USA, China and India exhibit strong tendencies towards inequality with economic gains benefiting the richest at the expense of the poorest sectors of these countries' populations.

This unequal distribution of income has major implications for children, with around a half of all children having access to less than 10% of the world's wealth (Ortiz and Cummins 2011). Thus few children and their families are in a position to take advantage of more open markets and the more fluid movement of resources across national borders. As Hevener Kaufman et al. argue, 'if it is true that some countries can no longer get to the starting line, children in those countries face the choice of migration or permanent impoverishment' (2002, p. 9). Inequalities are just as marked in terms of children's health. While I referred earlier to some broad global improvements, up to around 20% of children in sub-Saharan Africa die before they reach their fifth birthday whereas the figure in Europe is around 1% (WHO 2012). In the poorest countries such as Chad, Afghanistan and Somalia, the maternal mortality ratio is over 1,000 for every 100,000 live births. In Europe this figure is nearer 21 per 100,000 live births. While there are major differences between countries, there are also significant inequalities within countries. For example, African-American women are almost three times more likely to die in childbirth than women of other ethnic origins in the USA. These inequalities within countries are particularly marked when focusing on one nation that arguably has been able to take most advantage of the global economic change.

The liberalizing of the economy in China has generated major changes in the flow of populations within the country. I want to turn to this now and examine the implications that migration has for Chinese children and their families.

China and the case of the left-behind children

There is some debate as to whether migration is an inevitable feature of globalization (Czaika and de Hass 2013). Nevertheless, transnational migration is a persistent global feature, with populations moving en masse across national boundaries in search of work, protection from political and social persecution and escape from natural disasters. At the same time globalization has major implications for the social and political geography of a nation. In particular, globalization can be seen as the rapid industrialization of regions within nation-states, where there have been massive flows of economic migrants within countries which have major implications for the children of these migrants. I want to concentrate on internal migration and in particular the case of China, where migration from the countryside to the cities has become a major national and international concern, particularly for the children of migrants. In China the expansion of free market principles has been particularly marked. The 1978 Chinese government's 'open-door' policy ushered in a period of massive economic expansion, with the economy being 'internationalized': foreign investment increased by 850% between 1983 and 2007 and now more than 50% of trade within China involves non-Chinese multi-national corporations (Saee 2011). This has led to a major shift away from state investment in welfare and full employment with the earlier Maoist 'iron rice bowl' commitment to full employment giving way to a mixture of more contractual individualistic arrangements and more precarious informal approaches to the labour market (Kuruvilla, Kwan Lee and Gallagher 2012). Much of this employment has been generated in the industrial heartlands around the southern coastal cities of China.

This has had major implications for Chinese children and their families. Since the 1980s approximately 220 million migrants have moved from rural China to the industrial heartlands in the coastal south of China, generating greater economic and political inequalities between urban and rural populations. The practice of *Hukou* in China means that the Chinese population is registered at the place of birth, with rural migrants losing their residential status when they move to the cities. Thus mass internal migration has created a large disadvantaged population of those living in cities from the countryside but denied the citizenship status of those registered as living in the city (Luo 2012). Those living in the cities are defined as 'residents', whereas migrants are defined as peasants with limited rights. This latter group of migrants has limited access to welfare support, housing and schooling and is more likely to work in the informal sector, characterized by poor working conditions and pay. Migrant workers also have limited political representation with respect to the distribution of local resources. The children of migrant workers have limited access to schools, and schooling is generally of an inferior quality. In recent years migrant families have set up their own schools for their children, particularly in some areas where migrants constitute the biggest population. However, conditions in these schools are difficult due to the migrant children's lack of residential status. Biao (2007) argues that local authorities have now taken a far more punitive approach to these schools, with children regularly being excluded. These conditions have acted as a disincentive to migrants wanting to bring their families into the cities. The net result is that around 70% of children of migrant adults, around 58 million, and approximately 40% of all school-age rural children, are 'left behind', looked after by extended kin and, in a small minority of cases, left to fend for themselves (Liang et al. 2008).

The official expectation is that those left behind in the rural areas are actually 'holding the fort': with migrant parents temporarily moving to the cities in search of work, and the extended family mediating the negative effects of children's separation from their migrant parents (China.org.cn 2006). This is undoubtedly the case for many migrating parents, with around 80% of grandparents looking after the children of migrant parents. Moreover, the extended family is the norm in the countryside, with grandparents playing a much more formative role in children's lives. In economic terms most migrants move to the cities in search of better-paid work: around 90% of migrants with children send remittances back to the extended family. It is difficult to know whether these remittances have an overall positive effect on families once the negative consequences of 'absent' migrant parents are taken into account (Amuedo-Dorantes and Pozo 2010). Hu (2012) argues that the money sent back to Chinese rural families by migrant parents helps to mitigate this absence. But the general focus of the discourse here on left-behind children is more negative. While the motives of Chinese migrant parents are driven by a desire to improve the economic situation for themselves and their families, the separation of children from at least one migrant parent can be prolonged, with around 30% of children seeing their parents less than once a year. And, as we can see from news stories, there does seem to be some recognition of 'left-behind' children as a major social problem in China associated with high-profile cases of urban street children, and a range of developmental and social problems affecting rural children.[2]

There has also been an increase in research trying to pin down the kinds of issues that these children experience and are likely to face as adults. There has been a major focus on how prolonged parental separation affects children's school experiences and outcomes (Luo 2012; Xiang 2007; Yao and Mao 2008; Liang et al. 2008). Some of this research is comparing the educational and psychological wellbeing of 'left-behind children' with the children of non-migrating parents. In some cases there is statistical evidence to support the thesis that the absence of one or both parents for extended periods has a deleterious effect on rural children's wellbeing, in particular children's wellbeing in school. While the gender of the migrating parent is a moderating factor, with the absence of the migrant mother a more damaging factor than the 'absent' migrant father, the children of migrating parents among other things are more likely to assume more household responsibilities; their homes are more likely to be impoverished sites for their educational development and they are more likely to develop psychological and emotional problems that have a negative impact on their social and educational wellbeing (Luo 2012; Liang et al. 2008; Yao and Mao 2008).

Other research is more cautious: it is not always clear that 'left-behind' children's wellbeing is more compromised than the wellbeing of their rural peers in 'intact' families (Xiang 2007). The issue of left-behind children which focuses on the absence of parents obscures a more fundamental structural issue, a direct consequence of the rise of a market economy in China, that of continuing poverty experienced by children and families in rural China. Xiang (2007) argues that there are no significant differences between rural children from migrant and non-migrant families with both groups of children displaying a range of social and emotional problems. Luo (2012) talks about the quality and quantity of schooling being the most significant indicator of socio-economic differences between urban and rural families in China. One of the major reasons for the problems affecting all categories of rural children is the lack of investment in schooling in the rural regions, particularly at the earlier or 'basic level' stages of education. This has led to major problems in the paying of teachers' salaries with teachers themselves migrating to the cities in search of greater economic security (Xiang 2007). One claim by the UN is that China has achieved one of the Millennium Development Goals to halve the rate of 'extreme poverty' between 1990 and 2015 (UN 2013). As with all claims about broader absolute improvements generated by economic and political features of globalization, any progress made in improving the wellbeing of children and their families in China as a whole tells us very little about the growing social and economic inequalities between rural and urban children in China. We could say here that all rural children are left behind in the global rush with free market policies generating more pronounced economic and political inequalities between urban and rural children.

Political dimension

In turning to the political dimension of globalization, the liberalizing of the Chinese economy is not matched by significant changes to the political system. The tension between economic reforms and the *Hukou* as a local political system attests to this (Biao 2007). Yet, in general there have been some major shifts in political structures across the globe. The rise of nation-states, the coterminous relationship between territory and unit of governance, has continued with the number of nation-states increasing from 156 in 1989 to 208 by the mid 2000s (Cohen and Kennedy 2007, p. 127). While this expansion has led to an increase in the number of smaller units of political governance, power and political autonomy within these units has moved towards more international or global units of political analysis. There is an overlying shift from 'statism' to what Scholte (2005, p. 186) calls 'polycentrism' whereby political power and the machinery of government has shifted away from nation-states towards supranational organizations such as the European Union and the World Trade Organization. This dispersal of political power across nation-state boundaries means that political power has a more complex presence across a range of territorial levels, with nation-states retaining some of their powers but often having to rely on their links to organizations such as the International Monetary Fund (IMF), World Bank and European Union.

Various economic regional blocs have become more powerful politically such as the European Union (EU) and the North American Free Trade Agreement (NAFTA). States now have less legal autonomy with international law assuming a more significant role in judicial arrangements. For example, a range of European Human Rights legislation has become an important legal frame of reference now for many European states (Cohen and Kennedy 2007). Moreover, a range of non-governmental organizations (NGO) has risen in the past few decades with particular interests in the global environment. To illustrate: the World Wide Fund (WWF) is one of the best known NGOs working to protect the environment working with 100 countries. States often have to work alongside these organizations sometimes coming into conflict with them; for example, the French state clashed with Greenpeace, an independent global environmentalist organization, in New Zealand in 1985 over the sinking of one of Greenpeace's boats by the French navy and the killing of a photographer who had been on the boat.

What have the implications been for children of these global political shifts? First, following the rise of international political bodies there has been a significant increase in and expansion of international governmental and non-governmental organizations involved with children. In the former case the formation of the United Nations in the aftermath of World War II in 1947 was quickly followed by the setting up of the United National Children's Fund (UNICEF), an organizational offshoot of the UN that deals with child-related issues with offices in more than 190 countries. In the latter case Save the Children, which was set up in the early part of the twentieth century, was one among a number of NGOs that expanded during the 1960s in what was called the 'decade of development'. Other notable NGOs with a commitment to tackling child poverty are OXFAM and Catholic Action for Aid (CAFOD). These third-sector organizations have become a prominent feature of civil societies in many countries, setting up offices across the globe, and are in a much stronger position to take advantage of the rise in the global mass media in mobilizing their campaigns for greater global commitment to problems affecting children. Save the Children, for example, has bases in 29 countries and is actively working in 120 countries.

Second, in the past couple of decades there have been a number of legal and political commitments to children, including the UNCRC (1989), the African Charter on the Rights and Welfare of the Child (1999), the Dakar Agreement (2000) and the Millennium Development Goals (MDG), with the latter two committed to universal primary education by 2015 under the broader remit of 'eradicating poverty and hunger'. These international legal commitments are not binding, despite the role of the UN Committee on the Rights of the Child to audit the actions of governments. Much has been made of the unwillingness of states to implement the CRC (UN 2009; Lyon 2007). Nevertheless, as I go on to argue later in this chapter, they are particularly significant in helping to shape a powerful global conception of childhood as a global standard.

This global focus on children has resulted in some progress being made in tackling child poverty and increasing school participation. In the former case the aim was to halve 'extreme poverty' defined as those living on less than $1.25 per day between 1990 and 2015. Despite the continual rise in food and fuel prices in the past few years this has almost been achieved with a reduction from 47% in 1990 to 24% in 2008 of those in extreme poverty (United Nations 2012).[3] Similarly, there has been international and national attention placed on ensuring that all children globally are able to attend primary schools. There are significant regional variations in the proportion of children registering for primary or elementary schooling, with 76% of sub-Saharan children registering and 95% of South East Asian children. Nevertheless, overall there has been an increase in the numbers of Southern children registering from 82% in 1999 to 90% in 2010. Moreover, the figure of 76% for sub-Saharan children is a significant increase from 58% in 1999. Completion rates are similar with around 90% of children finishing their schooling, up from 81% in 1999.

Third, while there is no simple or necessary relationship between globalization and democratization, we can discern a trend towards countries becoming more democratic in regions that had been hitherto dominated by one party rule such as sub-Saharan Africa, Latin America and the Asian-Pacific and in the last couple of years in the Muslim states of North Africa (Melton 2002). These two trends are inter-related in identifying possible implications for children. Thus the introduction of a free press associated with democratization, a wider range of media and the greater significance attached to international organizations such as UNICEF have generated a much greater awareness of the condition, needs and to a lesser extent voices of children at global and national levels. Moreover, arguably international legislation on children such as UNCRC has introduced the concept of voice and thus more democratic practices to children. Fourth, this greater global sensibility towards problems and concerns relating to children as a sector of the global population allows us to reconceptualize children as a global minority group (James, Jenks and Prout 1998). Child protection issues have become global concerns: sex tourism, human trafficking and civil conflict are just three among a number of areas that have mobilized governmental and non-governmental support and resources. Childhood has become a major global political issue. Children here are conceptualized as a 'class', a separate sector of the global population with common interests (to be discussed in Chapter 5).

Political globalization has also had ambiguous effects. International sources of economic and political support have been provided for poorer countries and there have been genuine attempts to mitigate poverty in these countries. However, power at this level has also acted to influence the direction of national policy which has sometimes led to greater child poverty. Thus the influence of the IMF in instigating 'structural adjustment programmes' has led to major cutbacks in welfare spending, which has forced many families into the informal unstable economy and in some cases pushed children onto the street in search of work (Chossudovsky 1997). Countries in receipt of loans from the IMF have had to forego welfare expansion in favour of debt repayment generating high unemployment and increasing the numbers of children and their families in poverty. Moreover, in some respects the global politicization of childhood is also ambiguous. While international organizations have promoted a global childhood as the responsibility of individual states, these same political structures have promoted a singular conception of the global child which is at odds with the experiences of many children and their families in much poorer regions of the world. It is this particular issue that I want to turn to in the rest of the chapter.

Childhood as a global standard

In exploring the globalization of childhood in this section I want to examine the relationship between political and cultural dimensions of childhood. Globalizing childhood heightens the notion of children as a social minority group by locating children within social and political structures as a subordinate and disadvantaged sector of the global population. Nevertheless, in invoking a common global childhood the international political community draws on dominant cultural models of childhood. One particular focal point here is the participating child, arguably a dominant model of postmodern twenty-first-century society. An earlier modernist model of childhood reached its apogee in the mid to late twentieth century. What we see here is the welfare and schooled child (Hendrick 1997). The welfare state that developed in many Western countries in the twentieth century provided legal and social frameworks within which children and their families, preferably nuclear in form, were entitled to material support. Mass compulsory schooling introduced in the nineteenth and twentieth centuries in Europe, North America and Australasia provided sophisticated forms of moral, social and educational regulation for children. According to this model the individual child is carefully propelled along moral and social pathways before exposure to the world of politics and economics. As children gradually become more familiar with the world they are carefully incorporated into decision-making processes over their welfare and development. This is a powerful conception of childhood, a modernist conception but also a culturally specific model, that 'essentializes' and universalizes childhood (Prout 2005, p. 13).

There is significant continuity between modernist and late or postmodernist conceptions of childhood. At the same time two key global trends have helped shape a more nuanced version of the former: the introduction of the rights and participation agenda and the role that information and communications technology (ICT) increasingly plays in children's lives. While children's participation has become a more familiar feature of global and national agendas, a dominant conception of children's participation emphasizes the notion of voice and children's involvement in decision-making processes. Participation is predominantly *discursive* in form. Children are to have a voice in matters that affect them; this can mean anything from children being informed by adults through to shared involvement in decisions hitherto made by adults. The United Nations Children's Fund (UNICEF) draws on the seminal work of Roger Hart in their 2003 edition of *The State of the World's Children* series, subtitled *Child Participation* (2003, p. 4). Participation is defined as:

> The process of sharing decisions which affect one's life and the life of the community in which one lives. It is the means by which a democracy is built and it is a standard against

which democracies should be measured. Participation is the fundamental right of citizenship.

The second trend, the influence of ICT will be discussed in the following chapter. However, the rise of ICT has become a key feature of globalization. The mobility and speed of global capitalism, in particular the increasingly significant role of global finance, is aided by a complex network of communication systems (Prout 2005). While much has been made of the ability of children to manage ICT both at school, at home and during their leisure time, the role of the internet and social networking sites has the potential to both amplify and refine their voices (Livingstone 2003). Thus Collin (2008) emphasizes the participatory potential for Australian teenagers of the internet in connecting young people to political and civic initiatives, while Harris (2008) reports on young women's use of a range of virtual media in generating new political terrain within which politics can be contested. In the latter case this offers potential for younger children in their early teens, with social networking sites becoming a major forum through which they articulate political and cultural voices (Livingstone and Brake 2010).

In turning to the international policy discourse, one of the dominant features of the global political realm discussed earlier, there is a strong emphasis on voice-based modes of participation, which form the basis of a powerful normative model of children's participation. In the following I discuss three critical features of this conception of children's participation which are central within the international policy domain, firstly, its origins in the rights discourse and secondly, the regulatory role of adults and institutions. A third feature flows from the idea of the child as a future investment: the significance of participation provides an expansion of educational and developmental possibilities for viewing children as future adult participants.

Voice and rights

One of the key features of a global standard of children's participation is its association with the United Nations

Convention on the Rights of the Child (CRC) (1989). As many authors have now argued, the CRC has been the catalyst and subsequent framework for developing policy at national, local and institutional levels, influencing professional practice based initiatives for promoting children's participation (Percy-Smith and Thomas 2010; Landsdown 2010). A number of articles can be drawn on from the CRC in supporting children's participation rights, namely, Article 14 endorsing the child's right to knowledge and Article 15 offering children 'freedom of association and peaceful assembly', access to public space within which they can participate. However, international organizations and many powerful nation-states tend to focus on voice, and in particular Article 12, when referring to the participatory dimensions of the Convention. The emphasis here is on children 'expressing their views', and having these views being 'given due weight'. The CRC focuses on the child here going through an individualized social and moral apprenticeship with both adults and the state responsible for their welfare. While there is a growing critique on the implementation of Article 12, the CRC carries moral weight as nation-states are regularly audited by the UN Committee on the Rights of the Child (Lyon 2007). The 2008 report on the UK, for example, stated that in 'education law and policy' not enough has been done to encourage greater 'respect for the views of the child' (UN 2008). It is also worth mentioning other international rights-based documents. The European Union makes a fleeting reference to children's participation through the Charter of Fundamental Rights stating that children should be able to 'express their views freely' (2000, Article 24).

We discussed earlier the significance of NGOs as a device for promoting a global conception of childhood. A critical feature of the work of Save the Children and Oxfam is to promote conceptions of children's participation based on the CRC. A variety of projects, training manuals and resources have been produced by Save the Children with the aim of spreading the importance of children's voices across many nations (Participation Works Partnership http://www.participationworks.org.uk/topics/international-participation/save-the-children-international-participation-work). Save the Children, alongside other global NGOs, works alongside governmental bodies such as UNICEF in generating a much stronger global commitment to a more discursive form of children's participation.

Adult regulation

I will turn to the complexity of adult–child relations in Chapter 5. With respect to children's participation, we might speculate that the participatory child has a degree of liberation from adult regulation. However, the dominant global standard effectively extends the modernist model of childhood by providing more regulated spaces within which children can participate. The regulatory role of adults is pretty central to the CRC with Article 12 providing a framework within which adults, professionals and organizations can closely monitor and structure children's participation. Thus children are to be granted a voice on the basis of judgements made about their competence (the child 'capable of forming his or her views'). Further judgements are to be made by adults on the credibility of these voices 'given due weight in accordance with age and maturity' (UN 1989). Decisions about whether children individually and collectively have the capacity to voice an opinion as well as the range of children's discursive activities, and the forms this voice takes are taken by adults often within institutional contexts.

As was mentioned earlier, voice can take several forms, either through consultation where children's views are sought by adults, or contexts where adults and children together make decisions on issues that directly relate to children's lives. In almost all cases adults will mediate children's voices (Lee 2001). This is due mainly to the institutional nature of participation where adults are in positions of power and responsibility in relation to children. Again there is an increasing range of institutional contexts with children participating through their local civic authorities (Wyness 2009b), in terms of health care provision (Alderson 2008), in schools (Fielding 2006) and in social care settings (Kirby and Gibbs 2006). In all these participatory situations, children's ability to have some involvement in decision-making processes is structured by adults. There is no suggestion here that the form that participation takes is imposed on children by adults. In some instances children have agenda setting and initiating capacities. At a national level, for example, in Ireland the Foroige Youth organization encourages a range of smaller child and youth groups to participate more actively in policies on services for children, their families and communities (Foroige http://www.foroige.ie/about). Moreover, many participatory initiatives are based on interdependent relations between children and adults, with adults' success in working with children as participants partly dependent on the quality of relations that they generate with children (Wyness 2009a; Kirby and Gibbs 2006). Nevertheless, the normative modes of participation gravitate towards pre-existing institutional arrangements where adults have critical roles in structuring the form and direction that participation takes.

Future adult orientation

Another important feature of this normative global model of participation is the idea that the child participant is a future adult participant. While it is clear that many participatory initiatives are trying to accommodate the interests of children as children, these initiatives are also viewed as a rehearsal for future life as adults. First, the school dominates as a regulatory context within which children have access to a voice. Participatory activities within school often follow developmental lines with older children having more access to voice than younger children (Wyness 2009b). Children can be carefully and incrementally introduced to ever more sophisticated forms of participation as they move into older year groups. Thus an age-related trajectory which dominates children's school careers will influence the extent and form of children's participation.

Second, children's participation is often associated with children's citizenship type activities. These in turn are aligned to a social or citizenship based curriculum preparing children for full citizenship status in the future. While there is a debate among scholars about the extent to which children can be viewed as present day citizens, the policy and practice orthodoxy is that adults working with children are moulding future citizens, workers and voters (Tisdall 2010). This is the case if we refer to the position of UNICEF. Skelton (2007, pp. 171–7) refers to a chapter on democracy in the 2003 report *Child Participation*. There is a prominent discussion of participation as a means to providing children with a voice as children; there is also a return to what we might call a default position: participation is primarily an educational initiative that provides children with the skills and knowledge needed for a liberal democratic future.

Deficit models of childhood and participation

Drawing on the concept of children's participation I have discussed a model of childhood as a global standard. In referring to the latter it is worth touching on the complex nature of the North/South divide. Class differences run through both regions and arguably middle-class children in some 'Southern' contexts have more in common with their Northern middle-class counterparts than other children in the less affluent South. Globalization generates very different conceptions of participation within a Southern context. Lund (2009), for example, refers to the 'little emperor' phenomenon in China with the one-child policy generating an overpowering protective network within the extended family, with children's participation focused primarily on school attainment. This is compared with the very different lifeworlds of children in Sri Lanka experiencing civil war and natural disasters often having to assume economic and caring responsibilities. Within the context of the discussion in this chapter issues of diversity can be viewed in terms of a variation along a theme of problems; different types of deficit models need to be viewed against a powerful backdrop of the participating child.

As I argue in the following chapter issues of voice affect many Southern children just as much as children in the North. Nevertheless, a global conception of participation based on individual rights, adult regulation and future orientation connects quite powerfully with a twenty-first-century model of childhood found in more affluent Northern contexts. At the same time, international agencies and policy makers are committed to tackling a range of problems that confront children and challenge their material wellbeing in less affluent Southern regions, including absolute poverty, endemic civil war and major health pandemics. As we shall see in the following chapter, these conditions generate distinctive models of childhood. Nevertheless, international intervention is a critical mechanism in trying to bring children's lives in line with the model of the participating child that dominates Western countries (Boyden 1997). This in turn generates a comparative framework within which Southern childhoods are assessed in negative terms.

Yet in some respects the contrast between 'standard' and 'deficit' models is more sharply drawn by policy makers in the way that children themselves respond to these problems. Skelton (2007) refers to the way that international organizations are less likely to view Southern children's normal routine activities as 'authentic participation' because they do not conform to the individualized discursive activities found in schools and other legitimate public forums. Nor do these activities provide the educational tools for preparing children for liberal democratic participation later on in adulthood. There is an implicit distinction being made between material and discursive forms of participation by international policy makers. While voice-based forms are presented as a natural, educational and socially appropriate form of participation, material forms challenge dominant constructions of childhood, in particular, the nature of adult–child relations. These dominant ideas associate children's material wellbeing with their dependency. In referring to the way that the CRC has been interpreted by policy makers, children are provided for and protected by adults; they participate minimally in their own material wellbeing. It is worth referring to a discourse of needs here (Moss and Petrie 2002; Wyness 2001). At one level the perception is that all children are 'needy' in that children's material and emotional needs are to be met by adults in order that they develop towards adulthood. Childhood *per se* is viewed as a deficit version of personhood with adulthood as the global standard. At another level the concept of children's needs is articulated through a comparison between different categories of children and childhood. The Southern child in these terms becomes the 'needy' deficit child set against the normal child, the Western affluent model of childhood (Abebe 2007; Aitken et al. 2009).

In the following I want to illustrate this notion of deficit childhood and deficit child participation through a case study of child labour. Categories of problematic childhoods are complex and overlapping (McAdam-Crisp 2006). 'Child labour' is a good example of this in that it incorporates a number of other problematic cases of childhood. Images of the child soldier in war-torn African and Asian countries, and the moral and political rhetoric that surrounds these images, offer potent reminders to Western audiences of the disjunctive relationship between children and military conflict (Hart 2006). More mundanely soldiering is a form of labour, with children more or less exploited for their labour power. We are also less aware, but equally troubled by the notion of the child carer having to assume adult type responsibilities for their siblings' wellbeing in the absence of parents affected by the AIDS/HIV pandemic in sub-Saharan Africa (UNICEF 2006a). And again in a more mundane fashion these are children involved in hidden domestic forms of labour.

While child labour exists in a number of forms in Northern contexts (Hobbs et al. 2007), it is a useful case here as there is an inchoate global movement to tackle it as a predominantly Southern problem. The *worldwide movement against child labour* is defined as 'a loose constellation of individuals, groups, organizations, and governments focused on, and committed to, the elimination of child labour' (Fyfe 2007, p. 3). This movement has a strong representation from a number of international organizations including UNICEF, United Nations Education and Science Organization (UNESCO), World Health Organization (WHO) and the International Labour Organization (ILO).[4] The latter organization set up the International Programme on the Elimination of Child Labour (IPEC) in 1992. Through IPEC the ILO works with a range of international organizations, national government agencies and private businesses operating in 88 countries. The ultimate aim here is the abolition of child labour and by implication the strengthening of a schooled childhood with access to adult regulated participatory structures.

Despite attempts by the ILO (2006) to clarify the meaning and definition of child labour, it is still a heavily contested and politicized concept (Liebel 2007). Some international organizations take a more pragmatic line. The World Bank, for example, while committed to ending child labour, is nevertheless critical of the all-encompassing abolitionist position arguing that some forms of child labour are legitimate if accompanied by more structured support from local politicians, employers and educationalists (Fallon and Tzannatos 1998). Countries with large numbers of working children are politically committed to ending child labour. For example, India passed the Child Labour Act in 1986 in an effort to stop children from under the age of fifteen working. Similarly, several Central American countries including Nicaragua and Honduras have imposed age-related legal restrictions on children working. However, for the most part child labour is perceived as a major global social problem within the international policy realm. In effect it is often viewed as a deviant form or deficit model of child participation because it does not meet the global standard of a regular schooled childhood.

First of all, child labour as a form of participation is seen to be too adult like, compromising children's experiences of childhood and their ability to develop as children. Almost all international organizations distinguish between 'labour' and more acceptable forms of children's work. The ILO (2011) refers to the latter as work that 'includes activities such as helping their parents around the home, assisting in a family business or earning pocket money outside school hours', work that does 'not affect their health and personal development or interfere with their schooling, (and) holidays'. These forms of child work connect with the schooled child in that they are viewed as harmless and potentially beneficial in that they expand and strengthen the process of child socialization. In short, these kinds of activities are not perceived to threaten childhood. Child labour, on the other hand, 'is often defined as work that deprives children of their childhood, their potential and their dignity, and that is harmful to physical and mental development' (ibid.). In their most recent report the ILO (2010, p. 7)define child labourers as 'those children under the minimum age for work (15) or above that age and engaged in work that poses a threat to their health, safety or morals, or are subject to conditions of forced labour'.

One feature of almost all definitions of child labour is the absence of schooling: the United Nations through the CRC concur with the ILO in terms of child labour as a problem and argue that children should 'be protected from economic exploitation and from performing any work that is likely to be hazardous or to interfere with the child's education' (UN 1989, Article 32). United Nations Educational Scientific and Cultural Organization (UNESCO), an associated body, argues that the need to eliminate child labour is synonymous with their commitment to providing 'education for all' (UNESCO 2008). Child labour is seen as a critical obstacle in the pursuit of contemporary international attempts to introduce free compulsory schooling to all primary-age children through the Millennium Development Goals and the *Education for All* initiative. The schooled child here becomes a persuasive global benchmark for policy makers.

The notion of a standard childhood is also connected with time-oriented learning. One of the key disciplines of mass compulsory schooling is the learning of deferred gratification where the incremental acquisition of knowledge becomes an investment in the future, and the work that takes place in school bears fruit much later in adulthood. As I argued earlier when setting out the discursive form of participation, participatory initiatives function in the same way with practices in school and community rewarding children in adulthood with full political status. In recent years in many Western education systems there has been more emphasis on children's physical, emotional and social wellbeing *as* children (Wyness 2012). Nevertheless, by emphasizing schooling as a social and economic investment in the future, international and national agendas generate a sharp contrast between more affluent childhoods and the productive economic activities of children which are perceived to be more present oriented. Children's work here is seen to be quite distinct from the work they do in school because the focus is on immediate material survival, both for children and their families, the demands of poverty and culture shaping dispositions towards the immediate material needs of the present (Qvortrup 1994, p. 12). In these terms children's economic participation means they are less likely to be excluded from what are seen as primarily adult problems.

We need to be careful with a dichotomy that sets the schooled child against the child labourer. Many children combine work with schooling, with the former a necessary precondition of the latter. Moreover, empirical evidence suggests that child labour has a vocational dimension and a semblance of a career structure (Woodhead 1999). In many respects debates about the utility of child labour echo some of the concerns around the impoverished nature of vocational schooling in some Western nation-states. Nevertheless, a working 'mindset' is reported to compromise children's abilities to participate in school (Woldehanna et al. 2005). And international policy assumes that 'labour' has no long-term benefits, thus restricting children's life chances. This can mean two things: first, there is no educational or learning component. Child labourers adopt a present-oriented 'adult' way of thinking that is at odds with a 'schooled' approach. Second, any skills developed by child labourers, particularly the domestic work carried out by girls, restrict their ability to find work later outside of the home. UNICEF (n.d.) in a fact sheet asserted that 'too often there is little objection by families and communities to children working. Frequently it is felt that work is a better and more appropriate activity for girls than going to school'.

A second reason why child labour is an illegitimate form of participation is that work undertaken by children is often unregulated. If we take the example of one of the 'worst forms' of labour mentioned in ILO Convention 182 (1999), child soldiering, there is very little precise and up-to-date data on the numbers of children involved in direct military action. Despite many reports referring to around 300,000 child soldiers worldwide, the nature of children's involvement in war, the difficulties generating quantitative data in this field and its criminalized 'invisible' status has led Brett and McCallin (cited in Hart 2006, p. 217) to argue that the 'total number of child soldiers is not only unknown but unknowable'.[5] If we return to the broader category of child labour, the ILO (2006) claim that there has been a global reduction in the numbers of child labourers between 2002 and 2006. Liebel (2007) takes issue with this claim in arguing that the ILO's definition of child labour is too exclusive with much of the work that children undertake within the home not included.

Liebel (2007) also refers to the patchy and inconsistent nature of the sources from which the data are derived, claiming, for example, that in some regions the numbers of child labourers are actually on the increase. As with other problem categories of childhood, such as child carers and street children, in the absence of robust institutional arrangements through which these children can be systematically counted, measured, in effect become officially visible, there are major difficulties in structuring children's lives towards appropriate end points. This lack of precise knowledge and absence of regular adult control of children's economic activities can be juxtaposed with the precision involved in measuring and controlling the schooled child. Systems of mass compulsory schooling in Western countries are systems of control where children's use of time and space and the incremental distribution of knowledge are carefully calibrated.

A third feature of child labour as a deficit model of children's participation is that the unregulated nature of children's work exposes them to dangerous and unsafe working conditions. A key policy focal point is the ILO's Convention 182 (1999) and its immediate commitment to ending the 'worst forms' of child labour. These categories include forced labour, slavery and trafficking and children's involvement in armed conflict, and the sex and drugs trades. More generally, reference is made to eliminating 'work which, by its nature or the circumstances in which it is carried out, is likely to harm the health, safety or morals of children' (ILO 1999). Thus, children's unsupervised activities as workers open them up to being exploited by adults, and they are far more likely to be picked up and processed as potential and actual offenders by the welfare and criminal justice agencies (Boyden 1997). As various authors have noted the vulnerable needy child can quickly be reframed as a potential threat (Rose 1992; Donzelot 1977). The comparison with dominant voice-based forms of child participation here is stark. School and youth councillors exercise voice in relatively safe environments within the school and local community. Child labour, on the other hand, is perceived to be a more hazardous and risky pursuit for children, taking place in the more dangerous and less sheltered contexts of the street, the factory and the farmyard (Hesketh et al. 2006).

Conclusion

In this chapter I have explored the complex nature of globalization as it relates to children and childhood. While the rhetoric of a global free market and looser and more fluid links between nation-states has led to some improvements in children's wellbeing at a general global level, the first major theme of the chapter is that globalization in economic terms generates major differences in terms of outcomes for children and their families. I drew on mass migration from the countryside to the cities in China as an illustration of these differential outcomes. Chinese and Western commentary and research have started to pick up on the effects this allegedly has for rural children. The focus has been the social and psychological damage done to children as a consequence of the mass migration of parents within China. Yet in some respects the phenomenon of the left-behind child masks the underlying economic, political and social inequalities between urban and rural populations. An alternative perspective on the left-behind children in the Chinese countryside is that the partial liberation of the economy exacerbates economic and political inequalities in China with mass migration an attempt by millions of Chinese families to cope with the relative impoverishment of their economic conditions.

There are some interesting links between the 'left-behind child' and the construction of a normative global model of childhood discussed in the second half of the chapter. There is undoubtedly a rather messy fit between the life experiences of rural Chinese children and child labourers in other parts of the world. But there is some overlap with many rural children having to assume material responsibilities partly as a consequence of the absence of their migrating parents. Furthermore, researchers invoke a normative standard of the intact rural family vis-à-vis the family with one or both parents migrating. In one sense the left-behind child plays the same role as the child labourer in promoting a normative global conception of childhood which generates a dichotomy at least at a national level between normal and deficit conceptions of childhood.

In turning to the second major theme of this chapter, the political and cultural dimensions of globalization have generated contradictory trends in the way that we conceptualize childhood. On the one hand, there has been immense and intensive global scrutiny of the position of children, in the process universalizing childhood as a social and political space. Children in these terms are now more likely to be recognized as a social minority group. Following this through, we can see possibilities for challenging the ways that a global free market exacerbates inequalities between children at international and national levels. Despite political attempts to mitigate these inequalities through legal and institutional initiatives globally and the evidence from the ILO (2010) that child labour is on the decrease, children's minority group status means that they are the sector of the global population most likely to be affected negatively by global markets and political restructuring. Both trends generate the likelihood that children will take on more material responsibilities.

These political processes have generated a very particular model of childhood, a Western postmodern conception of the participating child. Powerful international bodies and national governments generate global expectations which inevitably lead to the majority of this social minority group being measured against a global norm. Various authors have talked more generally about 'childhood' as a form of cultural imperialism facilitated by processes of globalization (Nsamenang 2009; Boyden 1997). In this chapter I have argued that a more nuanced twenty-first-century version of childhood, the participating child, similarly appears through international policy discourse and is particularly marked when childhoods from less affluent regions become a global focal point. Moreover, this model of the participating child reflects much broader cultural global trends where less affluent populations have been subject to powerful neo-liberal and Eurocentric norms, which privilege rationality and individualism (Ling 2004). The structuring of children's participation takes place within a dominant frame of the individual child with the opportunity to play ever increasing roles in decision-making processes. As I have already argued, this is a culturally specific frame of reference that reflects the values and norms of more affluent

Western nation-states, which cannot be generalized at a global level.

This individualism also dominates the social sciences, particularly developmental psychology where the child 'is like the pilgrim, the cowboy, and the detective on television – is invariably seen as a free-standing isolable being who moves through development as a self-contained and complete individual' (Kessen in Morss 1996, pp. 43–4). The child here is viewed as negotiating various developmental stages en route to becoming a rational independent individual, a necessary preparation for membership of a wider individualistic culture. The power of this model marginalizes childhoods in less affluent contexts globally, we are more likely to find children immersed in their families, communities and regions where they participate alongside and sometimes on behalf of adults. In these terms children's participation takes on a more collective character. This implies that the participating child is one among a number of different types of childhood and importantly one among a number of different models of child participation. I want to discuss this diversity in the following chapter.

4
Childhoods: Diversity and Hybridity

The emphasis on global standards and deviant childhoods in the previous chapter focuses on the way that global forces generate a universal standard model of childhood. In this chapter I challenge the idea that these globalizing forces generate a dichotomy between normative and deviant conceptions of childhood by shifting the level of analysis and focusing on more 'localized' understandings of childhood. Fleer et al. (2009) talk about the dangers of reifying childhood as a global standard where more localized cultures and understandings of children's lives depart from this standard. I will argue that a more objective top-down approach can be viewed as an attempt to export Western conceptions of childhood with limited sensitivity to national and local understandings (Nsamenang 2009). Cohen and Kennedy (2007) develop this approach by also referring to 'bottom-up' processes of populations and communities both selecting from and adjusting to global forces and influences. Thus the way we experience and understand globalization involves making local adjustments based on a range of local cultural, political and economic factors. Robertson talks about this in terms of bringing the local and the global together.

> We must thus recognize directly 'real world' attempts to bring the global, in the sense of the macroscopic aspect of contemporary life, into conjunction with the local, in the sense of the

microscopic side of life in the late twentieth century. The very formulation, apparently in Japan, of a term such as *glocalize* (from *dochakuka*, roughly meaning 'global localization') is perhaps the best example of this. (Robertson 1992, p. 173)

Given the significance of 'glocalizing' processes, the focus in this chapter is on the diversity of childhoods, a range of different ways of understanding and relating to children and their worlds – a challenge to the previous chapter's emphasis on the global standard/deficit model of global childhood; deficit childhoods in these terms are simply different childhoods. In illustrating this approach, we return to the relationship between participation and labour and explore the ways that children in the developing world combine school and work in producing distinctive rather than deficit models of childhood (Hungerland et al. 2007). I will also illustrate this diversity with reference to a second 'deficit' model of childhood, the child as primary carer. There has been considerable international concern expressed over children assuming primary caring roles in the absence of parents, particularly in regions of the world where the numbers of orphans have risen quite considerably in recent years (Kendrick and Kakuru 2012). Associated with this is the emergence of the child-headed household, where children are assumed to take on a range of primary economic and social responsibilities in the absence of parents within their families. I will discuss the different ways that children adapt to changing circumstances that necessitate them taking on these responsibilities and hopefully in the process generate more positive conceptions of childhood. The aim here is to reinterpret the child labourer and child carer in order to highlight alternative rather than deficit models of childhood that incorporate discursive and material forms of participation.

In the second part of this chapter I open up the discussion of diversity by exploring the relationship between globalization and identity formation. Implicit in the discussion of the productive nature of childhood is the notion of agency, a dominant theme in this book, and the focus of Chapters 1 and 2. In this section we look at agency in terms of the different ways children draw on a range of resources in constructing more complex understandings of the self. The concept of hybridity is critical here: global pressures shape children's worlds, generating not distinctive cultural models and understandings, but more inter-related hybrid models where children themselves are more prominent in their constructions. We discuss this approach in terms of the different ways that children draw on popular culture and new technologies in helping them shape their identities.

Participation and diversity

In the last chapter I referred to the participating child as a global standard. The child here is characterized as having rights to participate as an adult-regulated discursive being. In starting to think about this model as one among a number of ways of conceptualizing childhood, I want to explore some concepts that help us to think more positively about child labour as a productive form of participation and thus open up the possibility for seeing children in more diverse forms. I want to focus on three areas here: gradients of participation, a broader conception of children's rights and the concept of children's spaces. First of all we need to rethink the dichotomy between discursive and material forms of participation. This will help to lessen the value judgement being made between normative (discursive) and deviant (material) categories of children's participation. We can see participation as an embodied process which incorporates both material and voice-based dimensions. Thus Jupp (2008) and Kraftl and Horton's (2007) analyses of Western conceptions of participation highlight the affective and physical dimensions of children's participation. There is an emphasis on how participation can also imply a more collective engagement and co-presence of bodies as participants become involved in events and processes related to decision making. Similarly, the actor network theoretical approach extends this merging of discursive and material elements as these events and processes involve the merging of people, places and objects (Prout 2005). While discursive and material elements are inherent in all forms of participation, we can analytically distinguish them as gradients of participation. Thus, as well as economic 'participation', which in working children's cases is heavily 'embodied' in economic production, we can start to plot a range of processes along a material gradient of participation. We can also run alongside this a parallel discursive gradient, with different forms of voice-based elements of participation.

Secondly, we can challenge the global emphasis on a discursive conception of childhood by reconceptualizing children's human rights. Murray (2010) differentiates between hierarchical and parallel conceptions of children's rights. In the former case children's rights to provision and protection are preconditions of participation rights. That is, children's rights are heavily implicated within a discourse of needs where children's wellbeing and welfare are determined and shaped by adults. Children participate once these basic needs are met. In the latter case children's rights to provision and protection run in *parallel* with children's participation rights. The latter means two things: children are involved in all aspects of their welfare – they participate in decisions with adults about their material wellbeing, and children have a say in their welfare as early as possible. Thus, voice becomes an integral part of children's material wellbeing. Alderson (2008) rejects any separation of these different categories of rights. She argues that there should be a more interdependent relationship between these different forms of rights, and that children should be actively involved in their welfare alongside their guardians and carers. Thus, for children's welfare rights to be effective, they must include an element of participation from children. Moreover, the effective protection of children must be a joint responsibility between the adult carer and the child. The abuse and exploitation of children can be both prevented and dealt with more effectively where children are both able to voice their opinions and concerns and take remedial action from a very early age. Thus, rather than coming after welfare, participation is a precondition of children's welfare.

In returning to the child labourer the issue here is both of child workers being involved in their own provision and having a voice in arrangements to ensure that their participation in this provision is respected by others. We can see here both the material and the discursive aspects of participation.

In many contexts children have to work in order to help provide resources for their own material wellbeing. Interestingly, some authors have argued that children's discursive rights are poorly developed in contexts where child labour is common. While children may be expected to take significant economic and family responsibilities, they have limited potential to express an opinion which may conflict with the views of surrounding adults. In Banks' (2007, p. 410) analysis of children's rights in Bangladesh, she argues that

> as children get older, increasing account is taken of their views, although adults display striking inconsistencies in their attitudes to the participation of adolescents in different aspects of life. On the one hand, the family and community expect them to act like adults – arguably overestimating their capacity – on matters such as work and responsibilities towards parents and other family members. On the other, their potential is underestimated and they are insufficiently consulted on issues on which they have a right to express an opinion, such as the course of their future studies or career, decisions regarding their marriage and other future plans. (Banks 2007, p. 410)

Liebel (2007) argues that this is a global issue in that the ILO has little interest in identifying the problems that child workers face from their own perspectives. Thus child workers' voices are absent within the international discourse on child labour. This may be due to the protectionist impulses of legislators not to complicate their narrative. Claims made by children themselves about the necessity to work do not square with a commitment to eliminating the category of child labour. While one could argue that listening to children's voices on their working lives might strengthen the international commitment to ending child labour, there is also an issue of legitimacy. International recognition of children's voices here is tantamount to accepting the possibility of children having some involvement in their material wellbeing. In some respects, neglecting the discursive dimensions of child labour heightens the material dimension of children's involvement and thus reinforces its deviant nature. Nevertheless, there is now a growing body of research identifying the complex and nuanced understandings children have of their labour (Bourdillon 2006; Invernizzie 2005; Woodhead 1999).

In recent years, working children's movements have been set up in different parts of the globe to provide more regulated environments for working children. For example, the Bhima Sanga was set up in the early 1990s as a way of improving the social and economic conditions of children working on the streets of Bangalore (Reddy 2007). Other broader based global groups also exist such as the International Movement of Working Children set up in 1996 composed of child representatives from Asia, Latin America and Africa. Children and adults involved with these organizations press home what working children see as a central right, largely ignored by international policy makers, the right of children to work (Liebel 2003). Yet this is not about children calling for more autonomy from adults, for built around this central claim is the right to work safely, the right to 'dignified' work and the right to work alongside access to free schooling. The central claim is for children to have their work respected and regulated by adults (Bromley and Mackie 2009; Liebel 2003).

Thus, just as voice is more prominent in 'Northern' institutions it is also a critical feature of organizations supporting children's right to labour in the South. While adult-regulated and voice-based forms of participation dominate Western institutional contexts, children are sometimes consulted on community-based projects that have important material ends. Take, for example, play-based initiatives involving children, where they are consulted in the design of playgrounds (Game Set Watch 2009). It might be useful then to move away from the dichotomous relationship between discursive voice-based participation that characterizes 'Northern' childhoods and the more deviant material forms that characterize child labour in the South within the international policy realm. The idea of participation gradients is important in that we are able to identify the interdependent relationship between discursive and material elements of children's participation and explore more dynamic movements between these two elements of children's participation (Prout 2005).

Third, we can reformulate child labour as a legitimate form of participation and extend the notion of discursive and material gradients by exploring the concept of children's spaces which offers a much more fluid notion of where, how and with whom children participate (Wyness 2009a; Mannion 2007; Moss and Petrie 2002). Issues of physical space are augmented with changing social relations between children and adults. The concept of space opens up the public realm to children providing contexts for more open and negotiable relations with adults. It thus challenges the notion of children's 'places' that restricts children's movement (Wyness 2009a). It provides more fluidity across geographical and generational dimensions. Within the context of the child-labour debate space means breaking with the school/work antinomy generating greater flexibility between the schooled child and the child labourer. In practice this means working with children as they try to negotiate routines and practices that allow them to inhabit the school and the workplace. International policy makers need to develop networks of support that provide working as well as educational opportunities for working children. Despite the need to avoid 'legitimizing child labour', UNICEF supports the establishing of flexible schooling which enables children to both work and attend school (Rosati and Lyon 2006). There have also been attempts to integrate work with school at national and local levels. For example, non-governmental agencies have set up learning centres with local employers, parents and children which provide more vocationally oriented educational opportunities for working children (Liebel 2007). Children thus participate more meaningfully across the workplace and the school where voice-based and material gradients are highly developed.

Child carers in sub-Saharan Africa

The child carer converges with the discussion of child labour in terms of being too adultlike and lacking in appropriate levels of adult regulation, creating additional levels of vulnerability. Moreover, we can see that the domestic and caring activities undertaken by children constitute forms of child labour. While this work is not commodified or recognized as work in strict economic or Marxist terms, as feminists have contended over the years, domestic work should be recognized as an important form of labour (Nieuwenhuys 1994). Like the child labourer the child carer has been conceptualized as a deficit model of childhood. In focusing on child carers in sub-Saharan Africa, the political focus has been on the absence or the lack of adult regulation, with child carers, an integral feature of a relatively new social phenomenon, the child-headed household (CHH).

This lack of adult presence provides a disjunctive conception of family life and therefore can be viewed as a deviant category of childhood. To borrow a phrase from Moss and Petrie (2002, p. 101) the child carer here is understood as 'needy, poor and weak', a victim of circumstances with relatively little agency. The focus on the CHH can be understood in two ways. First, there is an ongoing global debate as to what constitutes the norm in terms of family structure. In effect, both the extended family and the lone-parent family have become more globally popular (Pew Social Trends 2010; Bjorkland, Ginther and Sundstrom 2007). As we discussed in Chapter 2, there is some fluidity in terms of family arrangements. At the same time there is still an expectation that families are structured around a powerful generational axis with parents having authority over children (Cheal 2008). Second, within this generational structure there is a powerful expectation that caring responsibilities are distributed downwards in a generational sense. Care responsibilities as a resource are monopolized by adults and only distributed to children as they grow older. Children are expected to be cared for rather than doing the caring. In both these terms the CHH is seen to offer a weakened or distorted version of family.

The CHH is a particular problem in sub-Saharan Africa due to the combination of endemic poverty, civil war and the AIDS/HIV pandemic.[1] If we take the latter issue, the number of children orphaned in the region due to the pandemic has risen dramatically from one million in 1990 to 14.8 million in 2012. Around 80% of all orphaned children due to HIV/AIDS globally are found within this region.[2] There is some variation within the region with the worst-affected countries being Botswana and Zimbabwe, which have the highest levels of 'AIDS orphans' as a proportion of all orphans, with figures of 72% and 71% respectively, and Kenya and Uganda with lower proportions of 46% and 44%

respectively (Avert n.d.). Clearly the issue affects children irrespective of whether they take on caring responsibilities or have to take on the burden of other responsibilities within their families. Despite the endemic nature of the problem in many communities, children associated with the pandemic are likely to be bullied, stigmatized and isolated (UNICEF 2006a). Limited levels of adult regulation allegedly have fateful consequences for children's futures as adults. Parents provide love, support, emotional and moral structure as well as having the social capital that often provides children with access to schooling, work and other resources. Indeed, over 50% of orphaned children are adolescents and are likely to suffer 'psycho-social and economic distress' increasing the risk that many of them will contract the disease themselves through risky sexual behaviour (UNICEF 2005, p. 74).

Children affected by their parents' death due to HIV/AIDS appear to take on this deficit concept of childhood when they assume the role of the parent as carer. However, this is often a gradual shift in roles and responsibilities, as many children assume caring responsibilities when a parent contracts HIV. This can mean working alongside one parent where the second parent becomes ill. Children's domestic responsibilities become more prominent as both parents are infected. The concept of the child carer as a deficit model of childhood is exacerbated by the assumption that sub-Saharan African children are a category of children least likely to be in a position to take over from a chronically ill or dead parent. The children here are assumed to lack the material resources and the physical, psychological and social capacity to take on major family responsibilities. Children's caring responsibilities affect their lives as children: many of them are combining school with employment, with the latter a necessary precursor to the former and on occasion a crucial contribution to the domestic economy. Caring responsibilities potentially compromise their ability either to work or attend school. Many girls are likely to take on these caring responsibilities, finding it difficult to hold down regular work, forcing them to move into more dangerous unprotected work within the sex industry (UNICEF 2005).

The category of childhood here is also compromised by an alleged abbreviation of childhood as a part of the life course.

As I argued in Chapter 3, a recurring theme in national and international terms is the loss of childhood. As the children assume adult responsibilities, it is more difficult to view them as adults-in-the-making. In these terms children here are also seen as being out of school, out of family and thus potentially out of control, which has major implications for their futures as adults. The concept of futurity is challenged here, a crucial feature of a postmodern childhood. As one commentary from the *British Medical Journal* states: 'the potential for these children to form a large group of dysfunctional adults... could further destabilize societies already weakened by AIDS, has increased the urgency of finding an effective solution to the orphan crisis' (Matshalaga and Powell 2002). Kendrick and Kakuru (2012) refer to this as the 'social rupture thesis' where large-scale orphanhood has major implications for social order. More broadly, within the social sciences the absence of parental involvement in children's lives leading to childhood or juvenile deviance and crime is a perennial global theme (Muncie 2009). The issue here is how and whether a deviant category of childhood creates a generation of deviant adults. This has all sorts of implications for the legal and criminal justice systems in these countries.

Can we reconstruct childhood here? Firstly, we can say that the adult-like nature of the child carer in the CHH is too sharply drawn when compared with the dominant construct of family found within the North. The North/South dichotomy is softened somewhat. The changing nature of family in the North focuses on the shift away from a modern nuclear form, which provided clear lines of generational difference between adults and children with respect to roles and responsibilities played (Parsons and Bales 1956). In its place there are more diverse modes of family with more complex networks of roles and responsibilities stretching across multiple households. This also generates diversity in the way children experience and negotiate family life, with many children having to cope with rapid and fluid movement between households across and over time (Neale and Flowerdew 2007). As I demonstrated in Chapter 2 children with separated and divorced parents have to negotiate time and space differences in terms of who cares for them and where this care takes place sometimes on a weekly basis.

Moreover, the mid-twentieth century functionalist model of the nuclear family not only generated clearer generational differences, but differences within the generations, with mothers and fathers playing more gender-specific roles. Major changes in the labour market at the end of the twentieth century and beginning of the twenty-first have generated more complexity within the single 'nuclear' household with greater expectations that mothers work creating a 'time squeeze' (Christensen 2002) with families. This creates more fluidity of tasks both within and across generations and the potential for children to 'help out' more. To be sure there are still lines of generational difference, and in most cases children are still cared for by parents and other adult guardians. The greater complexity of their family lives in the North involves more 'egalitarian' generational relations. In effect, there is more recognition of the interdependent relationship between parents and children.

A second factor that blurs the distinction between North and South in terms of family structure and weakens the child carer as a deviant category of childhood is the complex nature of inter-generational relations in the South. Both children and grandparents have material responsibilities to varying degrees within the home. I mentioned earlier the significance of children's contributions to the domestic economy. Parents along with grandparents and other members of the extended kin will take on caring responsibilities and these arrangements often incorporate the caring roles of children, mainly daughters (Nieuwenhuys 1994). To some extent children's caring responsibilities are normalized throughout the network of extended kin.

In most instances the extended family is able to absorb orphaned children. As with the left-behind children in rural China discussed in the last chapter, the majority of orphaned children are looked after by extended kin. In sub-Saharan countries there is some diversity in care arrangements with variation in the proportions looked after by specific members of the extended kin network across the region. Around 40% of AIDS orphans are looked after by grandparents in Tanzania, 60% of orphans are looked after by grandparents in Namibia and Zimbabwe but around 57% of orphans are looked after by other relatives including aunts and uncles in Burkina Faso (UNICEF 2006b). However, in an early discussion of the effects of the pandemic on children in Zimbabwe, the country with the highest proportion of AIDS orphans, Foster et al. (1997) argue that while there is an expectation that orphaned children will be looked after by extended kin, there is limited capacity now with extended networks stretched and less able to cope with the numbers of orphans. This is also the case in other countries within the region with major strains on resources being reported creating, among other things, food insecurity within many extended networks that had hitherto absorbed orphans (UNICEF 2006b). Germann (2006) argues that this problem of capacity is evident in the way that cultural rules of lineage have been adapted where maternal as well as paternal lines of extended families are now expected to take on the care of orphaned children.

There is a lack of clear distinction between the emergence of CHH as a social problem and the numbers of CHH on the increase, due in part to limited knowledge about the extent and nature of CHH. Germann (2006) argues that the child-headed household has emerged as a social problem in Zimbabwe, with around 40,000 children living in child-headed households. Tsegaye (2009) argues that it is now a major problem in a range of other African countries. The CHH has also become a high-profile global issue in Rwanda due to the genocide that took place in 1994. The civil war between the dominant Hutu tribe in government and the insurgent Rwanda Patriotic Front from the mainly Tutsi tribe led to the mass killing of around 800,000 people, mainly Tutsis. This led to around 10% of the population of children being orphaned with 45,000 households headed by children containing some 110,000 children (Pell 2010). Around 90% of these households were headed by girls.

Interestingly, there is no consensus among international organizations with regard to the salience of CHH and the extent to which they are on the increase. For UNICEF the CHH is not an issue and figures peripherally in their 2006 report *Children Affected by AIDS: Africa's Orphaned and Vulnerable Generations*. According to this report less than 1% of all households are CHH and where there are children within one household looking after their siblings on their own, older teenagers take charge with some experience of caring. This contrasts with the views of the African Child Policy Forum, an independent policy and research organization, which refers to 'a significant increase in the number of child-headed households' (Tsegaye 2009), and argues for the category of child-headed households to be recognized as a new family type, 'a form of alternative care and a "least undesirable" care option' (Tsegaye 2009). The report refers to key features of CHH in a much more positive way, such as the resilience of children and the strength of the sibling relationship. Thus the CHH becomes one among a number of ways for children to cope with poverty and the HIV/AIDS pandemic.

It is also worth reiterating that diversity rather than global uniformity is the key theme in this chapter and this is also the case when analysing CHH. While the focus of much international concern has been on 'unaccompanied' child-headed households, where children are left to their own devices, there are also 'accompanied' child-headed households where adult relatives, often parents, live in the household but are too incapacitated to take on the primary household responsibilities (Tsegaye 2009). Quite often the accompanied form of CHH becomes the unaccompanied form as parents die of the pandemic. There are a number of factors that can sway children towards forming CHH rather than being absorbed into other forms of households including foster homes and care institutions (Tsegaye 2009).[3] In many respects children are quite committed to setting up home on their own with their siblings after weighing up the alternative care arrangements. Children prefer to set up home on their own for the following reasons:

- Children do not want to be separated from their siblings; and CHH is seen by these children as an insurance against this happening.
- Children are distrustful of institutional care.
- Children want to keep hold of their parents' property and do not always trust extended kin to keep this property in trust for them.
- Older children feel they can cope with looking after their siblings and have the necessary caring skills.

- There are economies of scale when forming CHH where non-orphaned children move to the city for schooling.
- Children are more likely to want to form CHH where there is perceived NGO support for them.

There is also a gender dimension to CHH. In some cases, girls rather than boys are likely to be separated from their siblings. Girls are more likely to be in demand for their assumed domestic skills than boys. Girls are thus in a stronger position to move into other households as domestic workers. Boys are thus sometimes left to fend for themselves.

Despite the mounting concerns over CHH, there is an alternative developing narrative which focuses on the capabilities of children to take primary caring responsibilities. Research highlights the competence and capacities of children to manage and sustain a household in the absence of adults (Kendrick and Kakuru 2012; Mavise 2006; Germann 2006). Germann (2006, p. 152) talks about the 'remarkable resilience and resourcefulness of children' within these contexts. Children in these terms have the ability to recreate a warm and supportive environment with help from siblings and peers and the broader community. Mavise (2011) refers to children's competence here as being able to make informed decisions with others about their own and their siblings' wellbeing. CHH is often made up of two older children who take responsibility for the care and wellbeing of two or three younger siblings (McAdam-Crisp 2006).

Kendrick and Kakuru (2012) focus more on children's capabilities, what they refer to as their 'funds of knowledge'. Their ethnographic research into Ugandan CHH challenges the view that children's knowledge and understanding of the world always need to be structured by parents, what is often more commonly known as the socialization of children. These funds of knowledge are developed by the children in the absence of parents and provide a more positive conception of their lives and the lives of their families within CHH. The children drew on a number of strategies in developing these 'funds of knowledge'. One was the importance of staying on at school after the death of their parents. This was partly about their understanding of the significance of schooling for their futures but schools were also seen as an important source of knowledge in being able to access support and resources. Through the teaching staff and other children in school the oldest children in CHH were able to get help and advice from local agencies. The older children were also able to help the younger children with their homework. Second, children mobilized local support to help, find and prepare food and thus establish a basic level of food security. Third, many of the orphaned children had to move once their parents had died. As well as seeking out new peer networks, older children tried to retain more established friendships, which again gave them access to adult 'knowledge'.

What we see here through these funds of knowledge is a combination of material and discursive forms of participation. Children need to negotiate with adults this knowledge in order that they can provide for their younger siblings. While the local and global context impoverishes their ability to exercise agency, it is clear from this alternative narrative that children practise more discursive forms through the funds of knowledge. As was argued in Chapter 2, children are able to mediate their poverty and exercise agency. A combination of material and discursive forms is also evident in the commitments that children have to ensure that their younger siblings are provided for and protected with help from other adults and children within the wider family network and community. Children's ability to develop and draw on their social capital was an important feature of their funds of knowledge. Moreover, there is an emotional dimension to this participation here. These funds of knowledge were generated and drawn on by children as a way of maintaining and recreating concepts of family and, in particular, some continuity with the past when their parents were both still alive. The researchers identified the significance of family albums with photographs of family being passed regularly between different members of CHH generating strong emotional bonds between siblings. We can conceptualize these funds of knowledge as part of a more expanded space within which children participate in family and community life. In accommodating children's material and emotional work here within a broader inter-generational context where children often make rational choices with adults, there is a balance between discursive and material dimensions of participation.

Diversity, hybridity and identity

In some respects the universalizing of childhood globally has generated 'other childhoods'. In the foregoing analyses of child labour and children heading up CHH, these 'othered' or deficit models have been recast as distinctive and diverse models of childhood. However, they are not necessarily in contradistinction to the participating child as the global standard, for they contain many of the features of these childhoods, their commitment to schooling and their ongoing relations with adults within their families, communities and often international aid organizations. What we can see is the interaction of local and global forces, the pressures brought to bear on children and their families from states and international organizations, adapted and played out in a number of different ways locally through families and communities. Kesby et al. (2006, p. 187) argue that this generates 'local, hybridized notions of childhood'.

An emphasis on localized adaptations means that children have the capacity to use a range of 'global' resources in unpredictable ways. One crucial feature of these local adaptations is the commitment that children have to shape their identities. The global backdrop to identity formation has generated opportunities for children to take more control of their identity formation. There is still some debate as to the extent to which agency is prominent in this process: in England some have contended that social class and gender are still dominant forces that structure identity formation (Shildrick and MacDonald 2006; Roberts 1997). More fundamentally, there is an issue of precisely how fluid and constructed is identity given that it generates so much conflict within contemporary global politics (Bendle 2002). However, Nyamjoh (2002, p. 49) cautions against essentializing identity. In his analysis of African identity formation he argues against the notion of African identity

> as an attribute of birth, transmitted through the life essence of a black African father, and to be protected from contamination by the products of other life essences. Being African...is a birthmark and a geography taken together.

He goes on and cites Appiah in defining identities as 'complex and multiple growing out of a history of changing responses to economic, political and cultural forces' (op. cit.). Children develop their identity over time; it becomes a lifelong process of adaptation. Globalization provides complex trajectories through which children negotiate a range of social, cultural and institutional resources in developing a sense of self. We can think of these trajectories as hybridities, not so much trajectories in the conventional vertical sense, more an inter-weaving of the nascent self through a network of resources at local and global levels.

For some, a global consumer culture forms a backdrop to children's identity formation. Children have become more prominent reference points for major companies and market-ers with leisure and educational merchandise a highly profit-able means of economic expansion (Kenway and Bullen 2002). This has major implications for children's construction of their national identities. Langer and Farrar (2003) in their analysis of Australian children's national identity make two pertinent points. First the local/global relationship can often mean missing out the 'national' middle:

> The symbolic material available in global consumer culture contains little upon which children might draw to construct a sense of themselves as Australian. The 'generalized other' embedded in global consumer culture is arguably a pleasure seeking consumer rather than a citizen, and insofar as a civic culture is taken for granted, it is that of the United States. (Langer and Farrar 2003, p. 125)

While their sample of 8 to 12-year-olds emphasized Australia as a safe and healthy place to grow up when compared with the USA, their main cultural reference points were global, including US sporting icons, fast food outlets and Disney toys. There was little sense that the Australian children in this study constructed any sense of being Australian through the consumption of these goods. The authors take a rather pes-simistic line that the goal of consumption for most children was consumption itself.

For others, nationality still figures in the background as a frame of reference for identity formation. However, within the context of global migration this has become a more complex and often confusing process. Generational relations often play a role, particularly among second-generation migrant children. Children here have to negotiate their nationality of birth with their parents' nationality, where routine and common frames of reference within the broader cultures have little connection with either. Thus Moinian (2009) refers to the way that middle-class Swedish children (aged 12–16) born of Iranian parents view their identities as fluid, often refusing to conform to essentialist stereotypes associated with being 'Swedish' or 'Iranian'. They refer to situations where 'us and them' distinctions are made and felt; they can feel Swedish vis-à-vis their wider Iranian family, particularly where Farsi becomes the dominant language when visiting their extended families. They can also sometimes feel Iranian vis-à-vis Swedes with whom they come into contact. These identities are sometimes felt as being imposed on them by their peers and there is some resistance. For example, the 'Swedish–Iranian' sample often fall silent when talking to their 'Swedish' friends about their families. Thus the children's own very close relations with their families are seen by them to be out of step with the more individualist views of family often displayed by their 'indigenous' Swedish peers. These conflicts are overlain by more global frames of reference, neither Swedish nor Iranian. Thus the children watched cable television and sometimes expressed their affiliation to all things American. Interestingly, one boy rejected Moinian's questions about their national affiliation: 'as a matter of fact I love salami, pizza and spaghetti more than both Iranian and Swedish foods. Does that mean I'm Italian?' (2009, p. 38).

These more essentialist identities are also notable with reference to issues and relationships between nation, faith and ethnicity. Children often have to negotiate carefully their parents' ethnicity, sometimes having to assume more complex identities in different settings. Hall's (1995) sample of second-generation Sikh girls in the North of England developed different kinds of hybrid identities within different contexts. Importantly, the balance of 'being British' and 'being Sikh' reflects relative levels of power between the two cultural reference points. The children adopt a dominant British identity within contexts where being British potentially makes a difference to their life chances. Thus the children were 'mainly British' in school because the expectations from within the school were that they behave in a British way if they wanted academic success. The girls make the contrast with 'home'-based contexts such as family and temple where they had to assume a 'mainly Indian' identity.

Identity and popular culture

Migrating and non-migrating children all have access to a range of global media. Popular culture in the form of television, film and music provides an important repertoire of resources for children when developing their identities both in terms of expanding the range of material available to children and as an alternative frame of reference from their parents. In the latter case, television can be the site of generational conflicts with second-generation migrants critical of their parents' preferences for watching home-based television because it restricts their abilities to watch the host countries' media (Buckingham and de Block 2007). In the case of Turkish families living in the Netherlands there is some ambivalence among the Dutch-born children towards their Turkish parents (Ogan 2001). The respect they have for their parents is tempered by an exasperated sense of frustration towards them for their lack of interest in Dutch politics and culture. Most of the families in the study had access to satellite television with Dutch-born children watching Dutch television and their parents watching only Turkish television, with the latter according to the children acting as the sole medium for informing their parents of political and public events and trends.

Durham's (2004) sample of South Asian adolescent girls' use of popular culture in the USA is an important means of identity formation and at the same time acts as a barrier between the girls and their parents. Durham's ethnography of five young South Asian girls' developing sexual identities is a useful illustration of how adolescents generate a hybrid identity. There are a number of cross-cutting influences on these girls. While popular US culture provides a frame for interpreting family, gender and sexuality, the girls' families provide a different, often conflicting, set of influences. Thus the girls are particularly subject to familial restrictions in terms of access to boys, the kinds of clothes they are allowed to wear and the extent to which they are able to take part in conventional adolescent rituals at school. In the latter case the older girls refer to the difficulties they have persuading their parents to let them attend the junior prom.

> RIA: I know I'll go. I know I'm going to go. I know I'm going to go with a boy. But my parents are like, I don't want you to go because of what's going to happen after the dance.
> RESEARCHER: What do they think is going to happen after the prom?
> RIA: We're going to get all drunk and get a hotel room and have sex.
> MALINI: That is such a teenage movie stereotype!
> RIA: I know! That's what's in all the movies about the prom but it isn't what everybody does! (Durham 2004, p. 149)

There is an interesting generational difference in perception of conventional US popular culture and youth rituals. On the one hand, parents based their control of their children's movements on stereotypical conceptions of US teenage life. The girls, on the other hand, were very sceptical of these representations. For them the reality was often quite different. At the same time the girls consumed a range of Indian popular culture such as Bollywood films and Indian music. They were sceptical too of the realistic content of these cultural forms. In the end they were unable to identify themselves with either host or home cultures identifying what Durham (2004) paraphrasing Bhabba refers to as a 'liminal' space between these two cultures within which they can create new hybrid sexual identities.

In more politicized contexts identity formation becomes a key arena for mobilizing political affiliation often drawing on a range of resources in the process. Children are still able to construct their identities from the symbolic sources at hand which may have very little to do with the political situation. Thus, while black South African youth's identities were shaped by the anti-apartheid moment in the 1970s and 1980s, they were also able to connect with very different cultural resources for very different reasons (Strelitz 2004). Children and young people can make important connections with a more globalized popular culture in helping to make sense of their relationship to conflicting groups within their communities. Thus a gay student makes connections with gay Western singers such as George Michael and Elton John affirming his identity within his local gay community, while a young black boy brought up in a community with active members of the ANC in the 1980s listened to mainly rap music imported from the USA, which helped to strengthen his resistance to the apartheid regime. Hip hop and rap forms of music have been used by young people in different countries in order to identify with a global youth culture (Buckingham and de Block 2007). Popular music here has resonances with these young people's experiences with their peers. At the same time Mitchell (2001) refers to popular music as 'resistance vernaculars', for example, hip hop and rap have been drawn by local youth as a form of protest. In the same book Urla (2001) argues Basque youth use rap and hip-hop and those local bands that draw on these musical idioms as a way of creating a 'Basque political imagery'.

Identity, technology and the virtual realm

In some respects children have been able to shape their identities drawing on material from within popular culture because popular culture has gone global and viral. The rise of YouTube and social networking sites, combined with a global telecommunication system that 'compresses time and space', has speeded up the process of identity formation and made it easier for children either to discard old identities for new or hold multiple identities (Mittelman 1997, p. 78). Moreover, children's access to information technology expands our conception of children's material participation, with children's competence with the latter enabling them to engage with others through the virtual realm. This realm has become an important channel of communication between peers and friendship groups. It has arguably become a critical means of identity formation, creating an online DIY culture, with teenagers able to present themselves in a number of different ways to their peers (Harris 2008; Moinian 2006). What is new about this technology, particularly ICT, is the way that identities are not always shaped, tested and compared in the presence of others. Hitherto, research on children, youth and identity has focused on the co-presence of children, particularly with their peers. The concept of the subculture or peer culture was premised on this co-presence in terms of the membership of children and young people in internally regulated peer groups with the membership of these groups both shaped and solidified through ongoing face-to-face interaction in and through these groups (Hodkinson and Deicke 2007). Developments within ICT have complicated this reliance on co-presence. The internet has produced new ways of communicating and expanded a network of possibilities for interacting with others and sharing and exchanging representations of themselves that go to make up social identities. While evidence suggests that ICT tends to reinforce pre-existing friendship and peer networks, there is also the potential to connect anonymously with strangers (Moinian 2006).

One example of this is teenage fashion blogging. Blogging is a popular medium for the young with around 50% of blogs started by teenagers (Chittenden 2010). Blogging consists of people at the end of internet terminals exchanging images, stories and other forms of interactive writing online with others at local and global levels. Chittenden (2010) worked with a small group of teenage female fashion bloggers (aged 14–18) mainly from the USA. She was able to identify the ways in which these teenagers were able to shape their identities online through interactive writing. The girls were able to experiment with a range of resources and images of fashion in relative anonymity but importantly at the same time gain relative levels of recognition from others which had implications for their self-image and self-esteem. Despite the lack of face-to-face exposure they were able to build up an embodied sense of identity through the way that they presented their images and fashions online.

Similarly, the online diary allows children to write interactively to their peers and in the process helps them to develop an ongoing dialogue between peers. Moinian (2006) discusses the role of Swedish children writing their virtual diaries in a more localized network of internet users or a 'web community'. Children sometimes on a daily basis produce narratives of their lives and their presentations of self were made visible and exchanged through these web diaries. These narratives often include references to their friendships, their schools, their families, their 'global' consumption in building up a picture of their lives and identities. While the online diary is another medium through which children are able to share and exchange ideas and thus help to shape their identities, it challenges the conventional notion of keeping a diary as something that is a quintessentially private form of self-reflection. The shift towards more public forms of diarizing reflects an important change towards more public and dialogical forms of inner reflection and in the process challenges in some respects the very idea of privacy and what we might mean by the private realm (Moinian 2006).

As with popular culture, children and young people have taken ownership of ICT in ways that sometimes bring them into conflict with their parents. Children have highly individualized and mobile access to ICT which allows them a degree of privacy from their parents. The greater mobility of privacy is clearly demonstrated by the popularity of the mobile phone among children, where ownership of a mobile phone is 'associated with privacy, freedom and security' giving children a degree of autonomy in terms of where and when they gain access to their peers, friends and parents (Bond 2010).

We can take another example, children's access to social networking sites such as Facebook and MySpace, which have grown immensely in terms of usage and popularity. The attraction of these sites is that they meet the demands of young people for greater privacy from adults yet in the process challenge the conventional view of the private as a physical and social space such as family. West et al.'s (2009) analysis of the role of social networking sites in the lives of young people identifies privacy not in contradistinction to a public realm but in terms of control of information about themselves. Children and young people have an ambiguous relationship to the virtual world here. They have private accounts or portfolios within a virtual public domain that they can manage in terms of who has access to personal information. Users can set their accounts as 'private' but this still does not stop others from accessing their information and the authorities are still in a position to monitor their use of private accounts (De Souza and Dick 2008). Thus the ever-expanding global dialogue embraced by children through their engagement within social networking sites is set against their desire as individuals to exclude certain people from this dialogue. For children and young people the issue is one of control of data about the self within a medium which becomes increasingly more difficult to regulate. West et al.'s (2009) sample was mainly concerned about parents having access to 'private' social networking sites. This does bring children into conflict with their parents. The latter seek to allay their fears that this new technology has insidious negative consequences for their children's emotional and moral integrity by encroaching on their children's 'privacy' (Livingstone and Brake 2010). At the same time children are committed to regulating the access that their parents have to 'private' data about themselves and their friends. De Souza and Dick (2008) argue that Australian children's use of these social networking sites is governed by a cost-benefit analysis with children's desire to present themselves in a positive light outweighing the cost of an invasion of privacy. If identity formation is predominantly about the ongoing exchange of cultural symbols then the rise of ICT and social networking sites both extends and transforms networks through which children construct their identities. Children have increasingly to manage a wide array of representations. The internet offers more complex virtual lines through which children and young people exchange and refine their senses of self.

Conclusion

I have discussed the limitations of dichotomizing childhood in two ways. In the first place international policy and a political discourse over the nature of a global childhood have generated a dominant and powerful notion of the regulated rights bearing future oriented child. This conception of childhood is taken as a global standard from which other conceptions of childhood are measured. In effect a powerful international discourse generates comparisons between the global Western standard and other deficit models of childhood predominantly found in less affluent regions of the world. In this chapter, through an analysis of working children and children with caring responsibilities, I have argued that we can view childhood from more localized perspectives and explore the interrelationship between global forces and national and local adaptations. A broader conception of children's participation, a human rights framework that integrates material and discursive forms of participation and foregrounds the concept of children's space offer more complex understandings of children's lives that cannot be easily categorized within a standard/deficit framework.

At another level the conceptualizing of childhood in dichotomous terms is evident when exploring some of the material on children's identities. The 'othering' of children takes place in and through the process of children negotiating social and often highly political environments. While children's identities are often shaped by overarching narratives on nationality, ethnicity and political affiliation, they do not always generate binaries between us and them. Again I have argued that the global context offers a range of resources for identity formation allowing children to create more fluid conceptions of the self. National identity appears to take on an added significance due to transnational migration with binaries being generated between different groups of children and young people and between first and second-generation migrants. Nevertheless, a closer examination of the symbolic identity work carried out by children reveals a more complex picture of hybridization with children able to present themselves by drawing on resources. The internet has both broadened and reinforced this frame of reference, challenging cultural expectations and enabling children to generate diverse and sometimes contradictory images of themselves to others.

While this chapter has drawn on two quite different bodies of literature, one of the common themes running through the chapter is the central role of children's agency in illustrating the diverse nature of children's lives, both in terms of highlighting the 'participatory' responsibilities of children in poor regions globally and the social and technical competences of children in engaging with others in shaping their identities.

What we can say here is that there are different combinations of material and discursive forms of participation being demonstrated by children which illustrate the diversity of childhoods globally. Rather than 'othering' more material forms of participation in less affluent contexts, what the discussion of the relationship between the global realm and identity formation demonstrates are much broader conceptions of children's material participation. In engaging with ICT and being fully immersed in social networking sites, children in both affluent and poorer contexts are both highly sophisticated 'participants' and social agents. We saw in Chapters 1 and 2 that this agency emerges out of relations children have with adults as well as technology. We turn to these relations more broadly in the following chapter.

5
Childhood and Generation

As I noted in Chapter 1, social constructionism has taken on the mantle of theoretical orthodoxy within childhood studies. At the same time political demands on childhood, particularly attempts to identify a global standard, have led to theorists arguing 'for a broader structural approach that situates children as a social minority group (James, Jenks and Prout 1998). Qvortrup (2009) argues for more structuralist approaches in order to refine and challenge social constructionism and although constantly changing, needs to locate childhood within more fixed social structures. In this chapter we discuss the ways in which generation acts as a theoretical method in structuring children's broader social positions. It also offers childhood studies a meta-narrative to bring it alongside other structural approaches within the social sciences. Firstly, we make the case for a more generational approach in terms of ontology; that is, establishing children's position within the social structure, which would move childhood beyond the ontological ambiguities inherent within the becoming/being dichotomy. Marxists and feminists make assumptions about the position of men and women and the different social classes respectively in terms of these structural positions being occupied by adults. In these social structural terms children simply do not exist until they reach adulthood. A generational approach, on the other hand, locates children

and adults within generational structures. A generational
approach then makes it less likely that the narrative of childhood is subsumed within other more established analytical
categories such as social class and gender. Secondly, a case
can be made for generational structures in terms of categorical differences. A categorical approach follows a similar path
to Marxism and feminism in that the generational categories
of 'child' and 'adult' are a priori and oppositional, allowing
us to differentiate clearly the position of children and adults
within the social structure. Structuralism is seen as a means
of providing social analysts with the conceptual tools to
locate generation as a dimension of social stratification and
thus another means of identifying power and structural disadvantage. In these terms children are conceptualized as a
social minority group, in much the same way as other disadvantaged groups. In this section we also explore a more
politicized theory of generation in terms of children's minority group status and how this draws parallels between other
structural approaches which emphasize gender and social
class.

In the third section I develop this idea of children as a
social minority group by exploring the problem of child
abuse. I will explore the political, cultural and economic
dimensions but propose that in order to understand fully the
problem a generational factor needs to be prominent within
the analysis. In the final two sections I move away from a
categorical approach to generation. I examine the possibilities
of the concept of 'age' as a means of creating a less oppositional relationship between 'child' and 'adult'. This is more
fully developed in the final section by focusing on more relational and interdependent links between adults and children.
When focusing on inter-generational relations the categories
of 'child' and 'adult' need to be created and reproduced
through ongoing relations between children and adults. While
a categorical approach separates children from adults, in
outlining a more relational approach, we will draw on representative research from three themes that bring children
and adults closer together: children's participation and the
ongoing role of adults; children working with adults; and
adults learning from children.

Children and ontology

In identifying the category of child within the social structure children's ontological status needs to be established. Jenks (1982) in an early 'childhood' text argues that children's ontological position is at best ambiguous. 'Childhood receives treatment through its archetype image: it is conceptualized as a structured becoming, not as a social practice nor as a location of the self' (Jenks 1982, p. 15).

Jenks goes on and argues that within social theory the child is always measured and assessed against the completed and ontologically established adult, in effect, children constitute an incomplete 'other'. Clearly, this book along with a well-developed corpus of work within childhood studies is critical of the view that children can only be studied or understood as human becomings rather than in their own right as human beings (Qvortrup 1994, p. 4). The earlier orthodox position saw children being absorbed within adult-dominated institutions as dependants where they had little ontological status. Children here are not of the social world: they occupy a space somewhere on the periphery either as transitional objects or as social apprentices.

In the first chapter we saw that one strategy for challenging this was to disaggregate the child from the family in order to illuminate children's agency. With respect to broader research strategies this has meant a shift in focus from adults mediating children's worlds to children themselves becoming the sole interpreters of their standpoints (Wyness 2013). In terms of children's positions within society there is a much stronger sense that children are fully immersed in the social world as contributors, agents and rights holders. As Alderson notes, the 'young [are] not simply learning and practising, they are living and accomplishing' (2008, p. 54). Given this status it is inconceivable that children could be viewed as anything other than social actors who occupy positions within the social structure. In these terms we can start to think of children as occupying a generational space within the social structure.

Categorical approaches

One approach, often viewed as a starting point for locating children within generational structures, is to view children and adults as instances or bearers of more abstract oppositional categories. If 'child' exists as a separate social category then the social structure is differentiated to take account of a generational dimension, in terms of nameable differences between 'child' and 'adult'. We can make the self-evident point that for children 'child' is a temporary status or category: children grow up and thus only inhabit their class for a limited time period.[1] However, the category or class pre-exists the flesh and blood child. Children inhabit the category on a permanent basis irrespective of their position within the life cycle. The category is, as it were, replenished with new children. A categorical approach views structures as constraints, or limits to what both children and adults can do. In experiential terms Connell (1987, p. 92) likens structures to 'being up against something', they both limit and shape the ways that we inhabit the social worlds. Social structures are constraints imposed on us by the nature of social organization. These are viewed as 'structural universals', limits that in some respects affect all children (Oswell 2013, p. 264). As Connell states, 'constraints may be as crude as the presence of an occupying army. But in most cases the constraints on social practice operate through a more complex interplay of powers and through an array of social institutions' (op. cit.). In terms of the categories of 'child' and 'adult' the dominant means of social organization is generation in that children are routinely constrained by their age and their subordinate status in relation to a more powerful population of adults. At the same time adults are also constrained by their generational positions. For example, concepts such as parental responsibility and the responsible parent, discussed in the first chapter, can be viewed as constraints on the way that parents relate to their children. Responsibilities become obligations that parents have to children which limit the ways in which they can socialize, nurture and care for them.

If we think about children in political, economic and social terms we can clearly differentiate them from adults. Thus access to resources and levels of governance are qualitatively different for adults and children. These differences serve to bring children closer together in terms of common features. Despite major differences in background, gender, culture and so on, generational status generates commonalities across the sector of the population designated children. Hill and his colleagues (2004) refer to a range of issues that bring children closer together: some of these have already been discussed in the book. Their focus is on children in the UK although this can be extended to include children from the affluent world in general. There is a general claim about the systematic discrimination of children: 'excluded from the mainstream of adult life' (2004, p. 90). This includes full-time paid work, political rights to vote and a range of legal rights. Moreover, these features of 'child' or childhood are common exclusions defined and prescribed by adults and organizations in terms of the concepts of children's needs. Thus adults have always been able to argue persuasively that children should take a particular course of action on the basis of adults knowing what is in children's 'best interests'. Children's needs are defined and prescribed by adults and justified through the invocation of children's best interests. Thus social science, professional practice and common reference points effectively exclude children from full access to political, economic and legal resources. In effect, adults have power to alter, shape and determine any conceptions of children's interests. Children's needs and interests are conflated. At the beginning of this century this paternalism has been challenged politically and academically with conceptual and political spaces being opened up to talk about children's own interests (Wyness 2001). Nevertheless, whether we are talking about adult or child defined conceptions of interests, the idea of children's needs or interests defines them as a common sector of the population.

Generation, gender and social class

The idea of generational structure has affinities with other more established dimensions of stratification in a number of different ways. If we look at the significance of gender in terms of a patriarchal structure, generation in some respects derives from feminists' concerns over the social structure of patriarchy and the role that gender plays in structuring differences between men and women. Feminism went some way to creating the male/female dichotomy with gender as a conceptual space to rival more conventional economic cleavages within society. Connell (1987) discusses categorical thinking with reference to gender and feminism. Here men and women are located within underlying structures or abstract categories: 'male' and 'female', which in some ways constrain men and women and generate a more dichotomous and oppositional relationship between men and women. Feminist thinkers have made links between a gendered structure and the position of children in the social structure in three ways. First, the development of feminism in the second half of the twentieth century uncovered issues of male control and power within families which came to be known as instances of 'domestic violence' (Delphy 1984). Cases came to light of women being physically abused by their partners. Although 'domestic violence' signified an oppositional relationship between men and women, it also opened up possibilities for examining other oppositional relationships within the family. Through the re-evaluation of women's positions within the family, the positions of children were brought to public attention with more focus being placed on the abuse of children within the home (Parton 1985). Child abuse was couched by feminists in terms of patriarchy – the power of fathers over their children (Hood-Williams 1990). The issue of domestic violence helped to bring the vulnerability of children to the fore, thus highlighting one critical feature of generational differences between children and adults, that the former's subordinate status as a dependant was not being protected by the latter.

A second point of convergence within feminist thinking ironically came about through a comparison of the subordinate status of children and the subordinate social position of women. Some of the earlier work in the new childhood studies made a historical comparison between the positions of children and women (Oakley 1994; Thorne 1987). Thus Oakley (1994) explores the parallel positions of women and children in terms of gendered and generational structures respectively. In particular, the historical position of women as inferior and subordinate mirrors the more contemporary recognition of children as dependants subject to the unilateral power of adults. A third linkage between feminism and generation is domestic labour. This has historical and global resonances. Early Victorian conceptions of child domestic labour in England were highly gendered with the work girls undertook defined in wholly negative terms as disorganized, 'natural' and only indirectly linked to the production of goods (Nieuwenhuys 1994). Here patriarchal and generational structures interact where girls are currently exploited through domestic labour because of their gender and their age. In a more contemporary vein Blagborough (2008) equates domestic labour with contemporary forms of slavery involving girls being exchanged from one family to another for economic gain. The girls' gender and age severely limits their life chances and subjects them to a high risk of economic and sexual exploitation from the employer family.

If we turn to economic material structures we can start to view children as a separate class. In economic terms Qvortrup (1994) has referred to the 'scholarization of labour' challenging the distinction between labour and schooling referred to in Chapter 3 and in the process emphasizing both structural and historical continuities with a working class subordinated within a class structure. Thus whereas Marxists emphasize the extant role of the proletariat in providing surplus value, Qvortrup (1994) suggests that this value is delayed while children are being prepared for future work within schools. The work that children undertake in the labour market both historically and globally has been scholarized, in that it has become a form of investment in their future as workers. Thus children's earlier labour in the nineteenth century was superseded by labour of a different form within the school with children viewed as economic investments in the future.

Children also on occasion resemble a social class in terms of their coordinated collective action. Research on children's cultures and subcultures has documented the ways that children are able to subvert the power and authority of adults through concerted action on the street and in the classroom. Earlier work by Willis (1977) and Corrigan (1979) identifies the collective strategies of working-class boys to take some control back from the teacher in the classroom. They can only do this by working together to subvert the norms and accepted practices within the classroom laid down by the teacher. Later work by Davies (2008) identifies Nigerian street children's collective action in generating a 'deviant' public image in order to gain a degree of distance from adult scrutiny and control. Qvortrup (2009) argues that similarities between social class, gender and generation turn on the idea of permanence. That just as men and women will always inhabit gendered and class-based spaces within the social structure, so children and adults occupy generational spaces.

Generation as a political dimension – the case of child abuse

In following Marxism and feminism childhood scholars position children within the social structure as a permanently disadvantaged and marginalized sector of the population. In locating children within the social structure they become visible in political as well as conceptual terms. Within this frame of reference children can be viewed as a social minority group (James, Jenks and Prout 1998). Children thus take on the same status as other structurally disadvantaged groups, such as women, the working classes and ethnic minorities. Issues of child abuse, child poverty and child exploitation have a global significance and differentiate children from adults in terms of the economic, social and political circumstances within which they live. In terms of common structural features of disadvantage we could refer to the idea that children by virtue of their generational location are more likely to be at risk from abuse than adults. Indeed, the very fact of prefacing 'abuse' with 'child' suggests a problem which can only be experienced by children – there is no equivalent category of 'adult abuse'.[2] Arguably child abuse can only be fully explained with reference to generational factors. More conventional political, economic, social and cultural factors are important in trying both to make sense of child abuse and broaden our knowledge of the kinds of children likely to be abused. However, children's generational status puts adults in a much stronger position both to abuse them and make it more difficult for children to come forward and claim that they have been abused. In the latter case this is partly due to children's lack of recognition as a political constituency. Children are not publicly recognized as a minority group. In the UK and in other English-speaking countries child abuse has been a major political and institutional problem for the past thirty years or so. Much has been made of the failure of child protection systems, particularly during periods where there has been a series of high-profile child abuse cases in both public and private settings. If we take the case of England and Wales, a series of physical and sexual abuse cases from the 1970s onwards has been followed by public inquiries and reports which led to major changes in legislation (Parton 1985). Child protection systems have been radically reformed twice in the past 25 years. While the 1-989 and 2004 Children Acts initiated major changes to the system, since the 1960s there has been a marked lack of political continuity in policy approach to child protection.

From the mid-twentieth century onwards the UK record on political welfare support for children has oscillated between a more supportive benevolent relationship between family and state from the late 1940s until the 1970s; a more critical association in the Thatcher years; and a shift back towards preventative state support in the early 2000s (Hendrick 2003). The new right approach in the 1980s and 1990s on child protection generated a more individualized and criminalized discourse with the state taking on a more punitive than supportive welfare guise. Among other things the mass media became more influential, highlighting a series of high-profile cases of sexual and physical abuse; there was a much stronger focus on conviction rates of child abusers and child professionals took on a more punitive role as 'forensic risk assessors' of abuse (Parton 1996). In the late 1990s this approach shifted with a move back towards more preventative collaborative work across welfare agencies (see Chapter 2).

This shifting political context has made it difficult to recognize child abuse as a structural problem potentially affecting all children. This lack of recognition has been compounded by a two-tier filtering system that renders instances and allegations of abuse invisible socially, institutionally and politically. At a broader societal level any increase in the incidence of child abuse or maltreatment in affluent English-speaking nations is very difficult to measure due to the hidden nature of abuse, what Jean La Fontaine (1990) in her classic study of abuse calls a 'family secret'. What we know about the extent to which children are abused is limited to official figures on child abuse or maltreatment which reflect patterns of reporting and recording of abuse rather than instances of abuse.[3] Thus a review of surveys of child maltreatment in the USA estimates that only about 10% of all instances of abuse are reported to the authorities (Gilbert et al. 2009). Moreover, once instances are known to the state a second filtering process operates through which allegations of abuse are gradually sifted out. Parton (2006) reports on a process taking place in the early 1990s in the UK and Australia where approximately 83% of all cases that came to light were processed out of the system by the time decisions were made about whether children should be put onto the 'at risk' register. Driscoll (2009) discusses this with reference to cases that came to light in England, basing her analysis of cases from 2007 to 2008. 'Initial assessments' were made on 59% of cases that came to the attention of the state or the Children's Services Authority. By the next stage of 'Core Assessments' only 20% of cases were still within the system and around 5% of cases instigated child protection plans.

There is an interplay of cultural and generational factors here. First, there are issues of credulity with reference to abuse by family members. This can be illustrated with reference to a 'rule of optimism' that operates institutionally and at a broader societal level. Accounts from children of abuse by parents are less likely to be believed where there is a widespread conviction that parents unconditionally love their children and would always put their children's interests before their own interests (Dingwall et al. 1995). Second, as we discussed in Chapter 2, family is recognized as a locus of privacy, with the concept of 'home' reinforcing this idea of privacy in that it makes emotional connections between family and a physical space (Munro and Madigan 1993; Lasch 1977). Parents are still able to construct boundaries which close off family from the outside world making it more difficult for accurate judgements to be made about children's wellbeing.

Thus parents' generational power is still discreetly protected by cultural notions of privacy.

We are touching on the 'darker side' of family life, where the structure of relations inside the family as a sanctuary generates more opportunities for children to be abused and for that abuse to go undetected. Concepts of family privacy presuppose a more refined version of the nuclear family with one generation of adults having responsibility for the wellbeing of the other generation of children. Thus, just as children are dependent on parents for material and psychological support, so this opens them up to being exploited by those same adults. La Fontaine (1990), in her early analysis of child sexual abuse, talks about abuse more likely to take place inside rather than outside of the family, which both hampers any attempts to improve detection rates and locates children within a complex psychological web of deception and collusion. There is an important relational dimension here – children are persuaded and sometimes coerced into keeping the abuse a 'family secret'. Children get locked into a psychosocial web with family loyalties and the maintenance of public/private boundaries operating within families reinforcing parental power. This often makes it more difficult for children to disclose the abuse taking place to those outside their families.

As I argued earlier there is a much higher premium placed on the concept of parental responsibility. The heightening of public scrutiny, a political focus on errant or 'irresponsible' parents and changes to the legislation have narrowed the kinds of powers that parents have in terms of discharging their responsibilities to provide for and protect their children. Nevertheless, the physical punishment of children by parents has not been abolished and there is still a powerful constituency of support for parents to retain these 'special' rights to punish their children as a necessary disciplinary privilege (Finkelhor 2008). There is little recognition among all family members that all forms of physical punishment are recognized as forms of abuse. There is still considerable ambivalence over the issue with parental commitment to ending smacking not always in line with parental practice in the UK (Bunting, Webb and Healey 2010). Gelles (1987) in his earlier research on physical abuse of children in the USA locates corporal punishment within the home along a 'spectrum of violence'. In this way the distinction between the hitting of children for educational and social reasons and the physical abuse of children is not so easily made with the former termed 'normal' violence and the latter termed 'abusive' violence. We could argue in Weberian terms that the 'state as the human community with a monopoly of the legitimate use of physical force' extends this remit to sanctioning the corporal punishment of children within the home (Runciman 1978, pp. 5–6). This clearly differentiates children from adults, and is all the more marked given that domestic violence against women was outlawed in England in the 1970s.

Part of this generational difference can also be understood in terms of children's victim status, which is qualitatively different from the victim status of particular groups of adults. Finkelhor (2008) from a criminological perspective argues that a number of factors differentiate children from adults in terms of the former being at a much higher risk of being victims of crime than the latter. First, they have much less knowledge and life experience than adults and are less likely to recognize situations that put them at risk. If we take the example of grooming, a process whereby an adult befriends a child in order to assault a child sexually: legal systems globally have recognized the risk of sexual abuse and have criminalized the process of grooming (Meyer 2007).[4] There are also now far more educational initiatives to help children identify grooming at a much earlier stage. Nevertheless, children's lack of social experience opens them up to being exploited by sexual predators. Second, children are in a much weaker position with regard to choosing with whom and where they spend their time. Their dependent status means that adults usually make decisions about the people that their children associate with and the places that their children inhabit and visit. Finkelhor (2008) makes the distinction between adults who can choose to leave an abusive marriage and children who have little clout in being able to leave an abusive family.

A generational dimension emphasizes the structural position of children as a population of dependants located within the adult-dominated and closed off confines of family. By virtue of their subordinate position within the social structure children are at risk from abuse. However, in trying to narrow down high-risk groups of children we might want to explore the relationship between children's generational position and other social structural positions. We want to return to the work of feminists and Marxists. In economic terms we might explore the relationship between poverty and abuse. With reference to the former, despite being one of the richest countries globally, the problem of child poverty in the UK is an entrenched one. Child poverty continues to be a political issue with governments since the late 1990s committed to reducing levels of social and economic disadvantage among the child population. In later years there has been some success with levels of child poverty falling by about a third between 1998 and 2012 (Joseph Rowntree Foundation 2013). At the same time the UK has a poor record in tackling inequality among children when compared with other affluent countries (UNICEF 2013).

The relationship between child abuse and poverty is complex, not least because abuse is an inclusive concept incorporating a number of types or sub-categories including neglect, physical abuse, emotional abuse and sexual abuse. There is, for example, some doubt as to whether sexual abuse is related to poverty (Hooper 2011; La Fontaine 1990). It is also worth bearing in mind that any relationship between poverty and abuse is mediated by the state. The intricate process of filtering cases of abuse referred to earlier is likely to identify families already known to the state. While there is no strong evidence that this filtering process reflects a bias towards particular types of children or families, the Dartington research on a small sample of 100 child protection cases concludes that lone-parent families are disproportionately affected and more likely to come to the attention of the state than biological two-parent families (Parton 1996). Thus 48 of the 100 cases focused on single-parent families, almost all were single female parents living in poverty. Thirty-five of these cases involved allegations of child neglect, the category of abuse that is most likely to be linked to poverty. Moreover, 65 of the families were already known to the social services and 57 of the families contained no wage earner. Having taken note of these caveats there is some evidence to suggest that overcrowding, unemployment, low income and poor parental education outcomes increase the likelihood of children being neglected and physically abused in poorer households (Hooper 2011; Gelles 1978). The Dartington research concluded that the emphasis on high-profile media-driven cases focusing on sexual and physical abuse distracts us from focusing on more generalized low-level contexts of abuse which were 'low in warmth and high in criticism' (Parton 2006, p. 65). Although not exclusively contexts of poverty, children within these families have limited material resources, and potentially are at more risk of abuse than their more affluent counterparts.

We might also briefly refer to the relationship between generation and gender. While there is some evidence to support the contention that physical abuse and neglect are linked to children's social class, the different types of abuse are arguably gendered. Crudely speaking boys are more likely to be subject to physical abuse, whereas girls are more likely to be sexually abused (Hooper 2011). If we focus on the latter, we can refer back to the elective affinities between the position of women and the position of girls. Girls as children and women are likely to be victims of sexually predatory adult males. In sum, children's generational position opens them up to exploitation and abuse from adults. We also need to explore other dimensions of social difference in trying to locate which groups of children are most at risk.

In the UK child abuse is a perennial political theme and there is potential to view children in these terms as a social minority. However, there are some obstacles limiting the idea of children as a structurally disadvantaged political 'class'. We have touched on some of these in terms of our failure to recognize children in generational terms as a disadvantaged group. First, child abuse in the UK has been depoliticized in social structural terms. While there have been some attempts to link these problems to systemic failures, they have been effectively pathologized and individualized, viewed as symptoms of dysfunctional families and subcultures (Parton 1996). Thus the generational transmission of habits and practices; the deviant practices of paedophiles and the perennial 'stranger danger in among our midst' theme obscures the analysis of these problems as endemic features of generational structures where children are systematically discriminated against on the basis of their location within the social structure.

A second problem with politicizing children's generational status is their lack of opportunity to organize collectively as a social class 'for itself'. In returning to Oakley's (1994) comparison between the position of children and the position of women, the minority group status of women was based on their subordinate position within a gendered social structure. The recognition of this collective status was a break from the past. As with the children's current discrimination women were also hitherto individualized and sometimes pathologized within the private realms of the home. This break was a highly politicized one with the women's movement and feminism in the latter half of the twentieth century to some extent shaping the political and economic agenda in more affluent countries and recognizing women's minority group status. Moreover, the issue of violence against women and in particular domestic violence was an issue raised by women themselves. In some respects women's greater visibility equates with politicization but in taking this forward women themselves had to make claims on the state for more equality. There is some evidence that states are indeed taking note of the position of children both nationally and globally. We have already commented on legislation in countries to bring children's collective status to the foreground. And the international realm has generated a relatively new status for children as rights bearers through the CRC. Thus while at one level this brings them in line with rights-bearing adults, we have a separate Convention for children with the Convention itself making it clear that children are different from adults with children requiring 'special care and assistance' (UN 1989, *preamble*). However, the parallel drawn between women and children breaks down in terms of a vanguard movement of children. While there are localized pockets of national resistance from children, witness the rise of working children's movements discussed in the previous chapter, adults in the main have had to take up the mantle of speaking on behalf of children. There is no equivalent to the women's movement for children. In Marxist terms children are unable to move from a position of being a 'class in itself' to being a 'class for itself'.

Age and generation

In some respects the categorical separation of 'child' and 'adult' makes it difficult to identify other positions occupied by children and adults within these categories. 'Infancy' and 'adolescence' and newer phenomena such as 'tweenagers' are established means of recognizing the age-related status of children and ways of marking out different positions within the category of child (Prout 2005, pp. 7–8). But there is little conceptual space for these positions within a categorical model of generation. Age becomes a means of refining the categories of child and adult. In Chapter 2 we touched on age as a means of distributing agency among the child population. In some respects agency became a more prominent feature of children's lives partly on the basis of the ways that children were socially differentiated along an age gradient. The concept of age complicates the idea of generation and the category of child. For it offers us a mechanism for bridging the gap between child and adult and at the same time refines the differences within the category of child. We can explore the relationship between generation and age by referring to the way that children's football or soccer is regulated in England. Community football in England is a very popular and well-established leisure activity for children. While much of the football played is informal and ad hoc, there has been a significant growth in the numbers of children and adults playing more organized forms of football. Regulation is significant here with the national body that regulates adult football, the Football Association (FA), setting a framework of rules and regulations which all registered adult and child football clubs have to follow. Thus children's teams and individual players from the age of six have to register in order to play in recognized competitions and leagues.

More recently a 'Respect' initiative was set up which provides a more updated code of conduct for all players, parents and coaches (http://www.thefa.com/leagues/respect). As with schools, community football clubs organize teams both generationally and by age. The concept of generation here is multi-faceted. There are clear distinctions made between children and adults in terms of how the game is played. Adults play according to globally defined and accepted rules such as playing on full size pitches with eleven players per side with matches lasting ninety minutes divided into two halves. The rules governing children's competitive football approximate to this but pitch sizes and teams are smaller and the length of matches is shorter. Despite the increasingly competitive nature of children's football, the one thing that marks out the culture and expectations of children's football from adult football is the idea that children are supposed to have fun, children are not expected and not encouraged to think in terms of results and league tables. Thus FA Youth Development Proposals state

> The flexibility of the formats allows the administrators to be creative and be able to meet the needs of children. Being able to be creative with formats allows the youth administrators to reduce the 'win at all costs' mentality most coaches have and give them the opportunity to introduce less competitive formats to youth football…there is no advantage to children to push them into over-competitive football and may harm their progress in the long run. (*FA Proposals for the Future*, 13 March 2012)

While it is important to define children and adults within these general categories, it may be worth drawing on the concept of age as a way of providing more nuanced links between the two categories as well as differentiating children within the 'child' category according to football regulations. Thus children as they get older and progress through a football club by age are more likely to approximate to the adult game. According to the FA organized football starts at the age of six when the children are in their third year of primary school. At this level they play five per side, and while teams belong to local leagues, there are restrictions on levels of competition between teams in the leagues. The matches last 40 minutes long, normally played in shorter 10 minute quarters. At the age of eight children are allowed to play in more openly competitive leagues with seven in each team and by the age of eleven matches more closely resemble competitive adult matches, with nine players per side and 40 minutes played per half. There are also age-related restrictions on the extent to which children's football is formalized in terms of competition. For example, there are restrictions on whether children's matches can be reported and where matches can be reported there are limits to what can actually be stated in reports with regard to match scores. Match reports are not publicly available for the under-seven teams; they are publicly available at under-eight level but reports are not allowed to mention the match score until they are playing for under-nines. Thus, while the major generational distinction differentiates at least in a formal sense competitive adults with non-competitive children where the latter play for fun, there are age-related nuances that link adult football to children's football. These are nuances within the broad generational category of 'child' but clearly demarcate the child category by age in terms of the extent to which competition can be formally introduced to children (Hendrick 2003). In one sense there is a categorical difference in that rules and expectations clearly distinguish between children and adults. In the case of football in England competition is a key defining feature of football that differentiates children from adults but at the same time draws the generational differences closer together on the basis of age.

In some respects children's football follows a developmental logic in that as children grow up and pass more developmental markers, so the organized football that they play takes on a more adult character. However, a developmental logic does not shape all age-related systems that move children from childhood towards adulthood. In turning to age grading within the school system children's age in school shapes children's differential status but does not always follow a developmental logic (Wyness 2009b). Children in many countries move from primary to secondary school around the ages of eleven or twelve. Children in the upper years of the primary phase are often asked by teachers to take on more responsibility and enjoy a higher status than the younger children in the primary phase (Deuchar 2008). Within the context of the primary school this does follow a developmental logic with older children accorded higher status because of their position within an age hierarchy that structures children's school lives. Yet an incremental increase in status in line with age does not always follow when children make the transition from primary to secondary school.

New recruits to the secondary school system drop down to the bottom of a parallel status hierarchy (Demetrious, Goalen and Rudduck 2000). Those starting secondary school are younger, smaller and less experienced than the other children. And on occasion they are excluded from normal school routines and practices until they have been inducted into the school norms and regulations. This is all the more inconsistent with developmental markers given that the transition from primary to secondary school converges with major developmental transitions as children move into early adolescence. There are general expectations in many affluent countries that adolescence brings in its train greater autonomy and levels of independence. This conflicts with the drop in status as children move from the 'lower' primary to 'higher' secondary school. Thus age has a more complicated social function within schools in differentiating children's status. Moreover, age as a means of structuring children's position with respect to the broader category of generation does not simply reflect a developmental pathway from childhood to adulthood.

Generation as relational and interdependent

A categorical approach presupposes structural differences between children and adults. While the introduction of other age-related categories provides some way of bridging this categorical distinction, there is little questioning of how children and adults take on these roles and positions assumed by these categories. The separateness of these positions makes it difficult to identify the ways in which children and adults relate to each other in terms of inter-generational relations. In turning to the relational approach we are drawing on more constructionist ideas which focus on the different ways in which children and adults construct these categories. Various critics see the categorical approach at best as a starting point for the analysis of inter-generational relations (Oswell 2013; Alanen 2009). Rather than see generational structures composing two a priori oppositional categories 'child' and 'adult', we need to explore the contexts within which we can talk about 'child' and 'adult' in generational terms. In some respects the potency of these categorical differences depends on how easy it is for us to locate all children within these categories. This effectively brings us back to a singular global model of childhood discussed in Chapter 3. We have argued in other chapters that children fail to conform to any single model or identity and thus we need to find ways of incorporating generational differences within theories that assume a diversity of models of childhood. One way of thinking about how the generational order is constructed over time and across space is to explore the ways in which both children and adults negotiate this order in and through ongoing routine practices. In other words, generational differences are premised on more interdependent relations between adults and children. What we are saying here is that a generational order is largely constructed out of broader *relations* that groups of children and adults have: the ties and understandings that both adults and children have of each other through media, policy and general rules and norms. These inter-relations bring the categories of 'child' and 'adult' closer together. Moreover, children routinely negotiate these ties and understandings in terms of more grounded flesh and blood *relationships* they have with others such as parents, uncles and aunts (Mayall 2002). I now want to turn to this diversity of inter-generational relations by outlining three trends and themes.

Children's participation and interdependence

In outlining this relational approach in more depth, I want to focus firstly on one feature of a postmodern childhood that has been discussed in earlier chapters, the participatory child. My reason for drawing on this model of childhood is that the research orthodoxy within childhood studies has shifted from a focus on adults mediating children's worlds and in the process muting children's voices, to children's perspectives being central to the research field. This is particularly the case in the area of children's participation, where the search for more authentic forms of participation has led to adults occupying more marginal positions and standpoints (Mannion 2007). There has been a much greater emphasis on children's agency and competence and the development of more autonomous spaces for children, which on occasion has led to adults being pushed into the background as marginal players within the participation field (Franklin 1997). What this has also done is to separate children from adults as oppositional categories. The child within this framework has been unintentionally isolated, relatively free from the powerful imperatives of adults.

In reflecting on the emphases on autonomy, and the movement towards adult-free forms of children's participation, I want to focus on ways that adults can be brought back into the analysis as collaborators and protagonists. Within a broader context of general trends within childhood studies this is a conciliatory move in bringing two approaches or two 'moments' together: the emphasis on the adult as the child's mediator and a recognition of the child's capacity to have a voice in what Zeiher (2003, p. 68) calls children's 'individual life spaces'. The aim here is to provide a more relational approach to children's participation recognizing the respective roles and positions of children and adults.

We might refer to Alanen's (2009) structural analysis as a useful starting point. A generational order emerges from children and adults developing and refining their generational identities in and through routine engagement with each other. Children within this framework have agency, the capacity to help shape the nature of relationships that they have with adults. In terms of children's participation Fielding (2007) refers to the concept inter-generational dialogue and collaboration as an ethical framework within which children engage with adults. His particular empirical focus is teacher–pupil relations and the establishing of student voice in schools. Adult–child relations are characterized within the broader structure and culture of schooling as more collegial and trusting. Cooke-Sather's notion of 'translation' is useful here: ongoing dialogue means the teacher 'can relate to students in a way that isn't an imposition; she can translate herself rather than focus on translating students; and she can support students translating themselves' (Fielding 2007, p. 305). There is genuine dialogue between both parties, and there is an ethical and political commitment to sharing information which implies a more interdependent relationship.

Wall (2008, p. 537) goes further in establishing interdependence as a basis for researching children and childhood. He argues from an ethical rights-based perspective when referring to 'a circle of responsibility to each human other' which incorporates children as both responsive to the arrangements made by adults for their welfare and implicated in these arrangements as active participants. This challenges the modernist concept of individual responsibility as applied to adults or more specifically parents, a top-down notion for fully structuring children's lives. A generational approach here can embrace the possibility of responsibility as a reciprocal relationship between adults and children with the latter able to modify concepts of responsibility. Woodhouse (2009, p. 820) from a feminist 'ecogenerist' perspective argues for the same form of interdependence in her analysis of the UN Convention. She challenges the individualism of rights and emphasizes their interconnectedness 'in demand(ing) that we recognize our shared interconnectedness and our shared vulnerabilities, as well as our rights to individual autonomy and privacy'. Within this framework we can start thinking about children's participation as a social or collective category, which becomes a characteristic of the concept of childhood as adults become more responsive to children's capacities as participants. While this is an attempt to synthesize a hitherto dominant model of adult power with more recent notions of child participation, this is not a conflict-free model of adult–child relations. Children and adults are involved in a dialogue where 'claims and principles are contested and contextualized, invoked and revoked' (Behabib, cited in Wall 2008, p. 92).

Institutional modes of participation encourage dialogue between children and adults as a means of heightening the roles that children play. They also open up the possibility of refining the identities of professionals working with children. Watts and Youens' (2007) research on the work of what they called 'professional pupils' in an English school illustrates well the notion of establishing an inter-generational dialogue. Groups of pupils were trained as pupil mentors in order to support and develop the capacities of student teachers who were in school as part of their teacher education. Pupils were learning a range of social and educational skills in and through their work with trainee teachers, while the latter were becoming more confident in their teaching abilities through the support from the pupils. These are not common practices in English schools. Nevertheless, they do draw out generational interdependencies with children's participation being mutually beneficial for children and adults.

We can also refer back to Moss and Petrie's (2002) concept of space discussed in Chapter 4. There is a material or geographical dimension to giving children space, particularly where children's use of physical space is highly regulated. There is clearly a sense in which children can use space to gain some respite from adult surveillance.[5] At the same time the use of space here comes close to Barber's (2007) notion of the 'engagement zone', where children and adults creatively engage and find new ways of utilizing these spaces. Implicit here are the ethical and social dimensions of space, where adult–child relations are interdependent, where this interdependence allows for children to be heard and where children work alongside adults. The role of the pedagogue is critical here. Pedagogues are typically used in some European countries as professional child workers to engage with children, and work alongside them in strengthening their voices as well as encouraging dialogue between themselves and children. As Moss and Petrie argue, this 'approach is relational. The child is not regarded as an autonomous and detached subject, but as living in networks of relationships, involving both children and adults' (2002, p. 143).

Children working with adults

A second way of illustrating the relational nature of the generational order is to explore the different ways that children work with, support and enable adults, particularly parents. The enabling role of children is prominent within families involved in transnational migration. In some cases as we saw in Chapter 3 migration can actually make it more difficult for families to stay together and generational relations are tied together in more distant ways. However, there are a number of ways in which migration engenders much closer and more complex inter-generational relations. If we focus on the role of Latino families settling in the USA after migration, Estrada's (2013) idea of 'American generational resources' can be used as a frame within which the nature of these generational relations can be teased out. These resources are defined as 'citizenship, English language skills, and knowledge of popular culture and technology'. Estrada argues that children have greater access to these resources than their parents with children utilizing them in helping their parents in their work settings as well as mediating between the family and the community. One feature of these resources is children's access to citizenship. Children by virtue of being born in the USA have formal political status unlike many migrant parents who are in the country 'without papers'. Estrada's (2013) street-working families ran illegal markets in Los Angeles selling fast food and on occasion children's citizenship status enabled them to support or protect their parents when families came into contact with the police or other authorities.

In turning to English language skills Orellana (2001) talks about the important mediating role that children play where parents have limited access to English. Thus children often act as translators where parents have to respond to official documentation. In some cases children translate for other adults within the community. In Estrada's (2013) families children's ability to speak English allowed them a more formative role within the family business taking on a range of roles, including preparing and selling food, taking control of the finances and acting as look outs where there was the threat of closure from the police. The final feature of these generational resources was children's 'access to technology and knowledge of popular culture'. Children had superior knowledge of the latest media and technology and had easier access to social networking sites. Children's use of smart phones was seen as a business asset giving the family instant access to wider markets and suppliers. Their knowledge of popular culture also put them at an advantage in terms of their market knowledge. Thus in one case a child was able to advise her mother on the most up to date and marketable videos and DVDs to sell on their market stall.

Interestingly, these roles were not always adopted by the children simply out of necessity or survival. Many of the children made the decision to help their parents out – for some children it was an optional activity with parents encouraging them to play, rest or do their school work. In generational terms there was no simple reversal of roles. To some extent the street becomes an extension of the home where all members of the family are involved in work. But children's involvement in the family business was combined with other activities and there was still a strong sense that parents had the upper hand assuming more conventional responsibilities for their children's wellbeing.

Adults learning from children

One important implication of refocusing on 'generation' in terms of interdependence is to rebalance the levels of influence that children and adults have on each other. The conventional view is that adults have the monopoly of legitimate knowledge that is incrementally passed down to children as they grow up. Children's dependence is largely determined by this top-down model. While there is no denying that this takes place given the regulatory roles they play in children's welfare, there is also a sense in which children's activities offer adults opportunities to reflect on their own social and political participation. Hart (2009) views the possible remaking of civil society through the development of participatory opportunities for children. In exploring the relationship between childhood and politics there is some recognition now that children are different from adults in terms of their interests and commitments particularly in terms of the ways that they prefer to communicate within the public realm. Children and young people eschew less formal political structures in favour of more networked associational approaches (Wyness 2009b; Cockburn and Cleaver 2009). At the same time children's scepticism of conventional politics converges with adult rejection of representative democratic approaches and a growing interest in extra-political issue-oriented forms of political action. Cockburn and Cleaver (2009) through their work with the Carnegie Young People's Initiative argue that children in the UK have a preference for less hierarchical and more informal ways of exercising voice. This not only challenges the conventional representative models of politics that dominate most institutional contexts but also offers adults opportunities to rethink the way that politics is conducted at local and national levels (West 2004). Children and young people's rejection of formal politics in favour of an issue-based ethical politics is something that has been picked up by adults (Harris 2008; Collin 2008).

A range of globally diverse contexts can also shift the focus towards more interdependent relations between adults and children. Here too we can identify a number of ways in which children's community or political involvement have had important effects on adults. One example of this is the intro-duction of Children's Clubs in Sri Lanka during the civil war (Hart 2003). The clubs were set up by the local children along with support from an NGO. Children ran these clubs but in the process helped to mobilize adult involvement in and com-mitment to changing things across their communities. One example of this is the way that children's participation in a range of community projects run through the school gener-ated more support from hitherto apathetic parents, with the latter much more likely to attend school meetings. Roger Hart provides another example, the Escuelas Nuevas in Colombia; schools run on more democratic principles that had a positive effect on the social and political capacities of adults within the surrounding communities (Hart 2009). Here we can see children motivating adults with the latter becoming more networked within their local communities. While these are localized examples and there is little strong evidence to support more national or global trends, they do stress the importance of adult–child relations in terms of how children's participation can often benefit adults. Thus by focusing on interdependent relations we can see how changes to children as a consequence of their participation can also have significant positive effects on adults.

Conclusion

Until recently social structural analysis of children and child-hood has tended to eschew variables that directly account for children's generational status. In effect the latter has only really been significant in endorsing children's absence from social structures. Age differences were a measure of children's location within individualized developmental trajectories which positioned them outside the social structure as social apprentices. The major impetus within childhood studies has been to establish children as individual social agents. While 'generation' has played a less formative role in developing analyses that privilege the social positions of children, it has helped to heighten the importance of children and childhood within the social structure. First, it provides social scientists with more nuanced conceptual tools for researching children's lives. Generation becomes an important variable of social difference and is less likely to be subsumed within other dimensions of stratification. Second, generation offers a substantive theoretical approach that locates children and adults within a generational order. In this chapter I have identified the ontological position of children, their location within the social structure and a starting point for analysing differences between adults and children. While there are clear links between generational structures and other dimensions of social stratification such as gender and social class, a key strategy within childhood studies has been to promote generation with equal conceptual status. Thus generation is promoted as an alternative analytical frame of reference for researching children and childhood with the same analytical power as gender and social class.

Third, generation has disciplinary possibilities in the way that 'childhood', hitherto relegated to the theoretical margins, now has a fuller body of theoretical ideas that allow for the conceptualizing of children as a collective social grouping as well as viewing children as individuals with full social capacities and political potential. An attempt was made to illustrate the conceptual possibilities of generation and the idea of children as a social minority group through an analysis of child abuse. There is a political and disciplinary imperative to separate child and adult in order to establish the importance of generation as an independent variable. The more categorical approaches offer a strategy for highlighting the power differences between the two populations that embody the two categories. However, a more categorical approach has also generated a demand to bring child and adult together:

we can explore more inter-generational approaches where the concepts of child and adult are built up over time through more interdependent relations between children and adults. Generation here becomes more a construct than a social fact. There are overarching structural constraints but we can think of these as relational, the categories of child and adult presuppose each other. We cannot talk of childhood without implying adulthood. Moreover, this interdependence is not synonymous with equality or symmetry – adult–child relations do not presuppose a relatively equal distribution of power (Sayer 1992). More interdependent relations offer a range of possibilities in terms of the qualities of relationships that children and adults develop together. This is the task for empirical research and in this chapter I have suggested a number of different ways or ongoing practices in which the generational structure might be ordered.

6
Childhood, Wellbeing and Multi-Disciplinarity

In this final chapter we reflect on the current position of childhood studies within the social sciences. While it is generally accepted that the study of children and childhood has become much more multi-disciplinary, there is still a question over the extent to which these disparate disciplines can work together to produce a genuinely interdisciplinary framework for researching children and childhood. In the first section we will explore a number of challenges and opportunities for generating just such a research framework. We set out the dominant multi-disciplinary position within childhood studies and examine the potential to move towards a more interdisciplinary approach. As part of this analysis we revisit the social/biological antinomy and ask whether the current dominance of the social realm within the new childhood studies can accommodate the reappearance of biological and psychological analyses, a precondition of any interdisciplinary approach to the study of children and childhood.

Second, in order to explore the potential for a rapprochement between psychology and sociology and a more interdisciplinary approach, we examine some of the children's 'wellbeing' literature, particularly with respect to the challenges that children face in the developing world (Camfield et al. 2009). The concept of children's wellbeing is a contested one, not least because it covers the social, emotional and material aspects of children's lives. In doing so it provides us with a context within which we can explore work done with children from a number of disciplinary vantages. Moreover, it gives us the opportunity to examine the potential for an interdisciplinary approach to improve our understanding of children's wellbeing. While international organizations draw on a medical/psychological model in constructing deficit models of childhood, the work of anthropologists and sociologists provides more contextual data and broadens the number of vantage points for understanding the position of children in the developing world (Boyden and de Berry 2004). In the third part of the chapter we explore the way that various agencies within welfare systems in many affluent countries have the potential to work more closely together in offering more holistic conceptions of childhood. While we might continue to question the extent to which health, education and welfare professionals work together in practice to meet the many challenges that children and their families face, there is a stronger political agenda for inter-agency work with children within the public realm. We will discuss the implications this has for working with children and families and explore the parallels between interdisciplinary and inter-agency approaches. In the final section of the chapter I briefly assess the relationship between the expanding fields of childhood at academic and institutional levels.

Childhood as a multi-disciplinary field

In the previous chapter I argued that a focus on generation as a category of analysis and dimension of social stratification suggested that childhood studies had achieved a degree of theoretical maturity; childhood studies had as it were grown up. Latterly, childhood studies have become much more self-conscious, with the potential for interdisciplinary work within the field a critical feature of this self-reflection. For example, in an edition of *Children's Geographies* (2010, 8 (2)), a highly rated journal with the social sciences, a number of authors have debated the potential of and drawbacks to an interdisciplinary approach to childhood. Throughout this book I have referred to a number of different disciplinary interests within the field of childhood studies and noted that these interests converge around a number of themes and issues. There is, as it were, little doubt that childhood is a multi-disciplinary field, in that a range of disciplines take an interest in the nature of children and childhood. A demand for a multi-disciplinary approach reflects the rising significance of childhood. Issues of growing up, inter-generational relations and the globalized nature of childhood are more pressing and complex as children and those living with and working with children live through rapidly changing and diverse contexts (Korbin 2010). If we return to the journal *Children's Geographies* there is ample space within which a range of disciplines can develop their conceptual and empirical interests in children and childhood. While the focus is on geography – children's use of 'space, place and spatiality' – there are numerous articles that incorporate these themes broadly focusing on sociological, anthropological and historical aspects of childhood. Furthermore, the journal is a reference point now for methodological and theoretical frameworks drawn on by academics in a number of different disciplines.[1]

However, when exploring the relationship between these disciplines, indeed, examining the possibilities of any kind of productive relationship between these disciplines there is much less consensus. On the one hand, interdisciplinarity is viewed as an important means of pushing the boundaries of knowledge, of generating new theoretical approaches and innovative methodologies. Importantly, to look at an idea or concept from outside your own discipline is to reflect on the limits and assumptions within your own discipline (Alanen 2012). However, the dominant rationale for an interdisciplinary approach is its utility in solving a range of global problems. For childhood studies this means providing a more holistic and inclusive approach to the problems and issues facing children. At one level an interdisciplinary approach to poverty, maltreatment or inter-generational conflict is part of a continuing modernist project that aims to tackle these problems. As we argued in Chapter 4 the HIV/AIDS pandemic has had a cataclysmic effect on children and their families. The economic, social and psychological ramifications of this cannot be adequately understood within a single disciplinary framework. We might anticipate an interdisciplinary approach having more purchase on this problem. Alanen (2012, p. 49), in reviewing the possibilities of an interdisciplinary approach, talks generally about what this might mean.

> The recognition is that childhood and 'the child' are indeed complex phenomena; understanding them properly, and not just partially, compels any disciplinarian to consult researchers from other disciplinary fields, and to develop efficient forms of communication and collaboration with them. The goal would be to integrate the central guiding vision(s) of the social study of childhood with compatible notions of children and childhood originating in other major disciplines concerned with children: an integrated, overarching framework for interdisciplinary childhood research.

Korbin (2010) puts forward a framework for ensuring that childhood research is interdisciplinary, with an emphasis on disciplines working together from the beginning through to the end of the research process. This framework includes a number of principles: the involvement of all disciplines in the framing of research questions, theoretical and methodological sharing, applying for funding at this meta-disciplinary level, research training in interdisciplinary work and finally writing up and disseminating work collectively. However, what on the surface appear to be interdisciplinary frameworks are often multi-disciplinary in practice. The disciplinary silos are relatively intact as a range of different disciplines come together to tackle an issue but effectively work on those issues within their silos (Alanen 2012). In some respects there may be a genuine attempt to conceptualize and develop research methodologies as a means of generating data from across a range of disciplines. But the research processes and outcomes may be multiple and parallel, with the different disciplines only intermittently crossing each other's research pathways.

Others are sceptical of interdisciplinarity in terms of principle as well as practice. Cook (2010) rejects the very idea of childhood as an interdisciplinary focus if it means convergence at the levels suggested by Korbin, equating this approach with childhood as a 'meta-discipline'. Cook (2010) poses a number of questions: how many disciplines working together does it take before it becomes interdisciplinary? Is interdisciplinarity a means of arriving at definable unarguable conclusions? Other questions are also pertinent: can and should sufficient numbers of researchers from disparate disciplines agree on the questions that need to be asked before undertaking the research? Cook (2010) argues that there are too many obstacles to disciplines being able to converge on definitive answers to questions posed. There are difficulties in arguing for a consensus over child-related problems to be tackled, particularly where there is still little consensus over the global meaning of childhood. A postmodernist conception of childhood fragments any modernist consensus. Issues of diversity in terms of the meaning of childhood as well as discourses that locate the problems that children experience become the basis for discussions across a range of disciplines rather than a starting point for working together. In effect, the 'problem of childhood' is problematized rather than childhood itself (Hacking 1991). Cook (2010) argues for multi- or 'cross-disciplinary' approaches where disciplinary differences are embraced and where these differences become the basis for an ongoing interchange of ideas about the nature of childhood. In effect, what is being argued here is the establishing of strong disciplinary principles and ideas as a means of generating dialogue between the various disciplines (Prout 2005). The best we might hope for are well established disciplines with strong commitments to working on child-related themes and areas with an awareness and some understanding of the language and practices of other disciplines with an interest in children and childhood. Moreover, this cross-disciplinary awareness operates on an ad hoc basis where disciplines come together in order to tackle child-related problems and where there is some consensus over premises, methodologies and research practices (Barrett 2012).

In some respects the issue of multi- or cross-disciplinarity is crucial when we explore attempts to bring biology back into the analysis of children and childhood. In Chapter 1 I referred to the importance of anthropology, geography and history in the study of childhood. Within the more general field of childhood studies there seem to be far fewer discordant relations between these disciplines and my own discipline of sociology than between these 'social and historical' disciplines and the studies of biology and psychology. If we refer back to Alanen's definition of an interdisciplinary approach, it is clear that an emphasis on the 'social studies of childhood' as a basis for interdisciplinary work implies that psychology plays at worst a negligible part, and at best a subordinate role within this framework. In turning to the relationship between psychology/biology and sociology there is still limited dialogue (Prout 2005). Lee and Motzkau (2011) and Prout (2005) refer to a still dominant bio-social dualism. The challenges to a hitherto dominant developmental orthodoxy within childhood studies have generated a much stronger emphasis on the social and cultural dimensions of childhood with social constructionism attempting to usurp developmentalism as a theoretical orthodoxy within childhood studies. Issues of ontology and epistemology are significant: is childhood biologically driven or socially constructed? Are theories of child development more compelling than work on contexts within which child development research is situated?

In some respects this bio-social dualism was not one of the key determinants of the new sociology of childhood as formulated by James and Prout (1997). For the 'old' sociology of structural functionalism was located similarly with developmental psychology as part of a dominant frame that universalized childhood, providing us with a modernist conception of childhood discussed in Chapter 3. Thus the dominant figures of the social and biological paradigms, Parsons and Piaget respectively, were similar in their insistence that children were incompetent and a-social and had to be brought into the world with the overarching support of adults.[2] Children's futures as adults were to be harnessed as an instance of bio-social power (Ryan 2012). Moreover, this bio-social power was the basis of the work of more historical figures within the history of childhood, such as Rousseau. Ryan argues that children have always been treated historically as bio-social entities in the way that they were conceptualized as projects of nature to be tamed, shaped and regulated by social forces for future purposes. In some respects then this bio-social *dualism* is a relatively recent phenomenon.

One way of exploring a bio-social nexus rather than a bio-social dualism is to assess the relationship between what

Bottcher (2009) terms children's neurobiological constraints and localized social and institutional forces. Bottcher (2009) takes the case of two children with cerebral palsy, a particular form of neurological constraint. In conventional terms we tend to think of this as biological forces constraining children's thinking or cognitive functions and thus their capacity to interact with others socially. Bottcher (2009) adopts a more socio-cultural approach to this 'problem' and argues that the ongoing dynamic nature of neural connections within the brain affects all children. Importantly, these neural connections interact with the social and cultural worlds of all children in different ways. There is thus a more dialectical relationship between the individual child interacting with his or her social environment and cognitive development. The quality of social relations a child has affects the development of children's neurological systems which in turn shapes the child's relationship to his or her environment. In relation to the children with cerebral palsy, the ways that these children's neural networks interact with their environments can be differentiated from children without learning disabilities' cognitive capacities along a spectrum of difference rather than differentiated in any qualitative or categorical way.

One area where biological research has been critical with respect to childhood is brain development in infancy. This has been part of a much broader shift in research focus in the 1960s towards what Abi-Rached and Rose call the 'neuro-molecular gaze' (2010). The focus on children's neurological growth gained momentum in the USA in the 1990s and in the UK in the 2000s (Blakemore and Frith 2005). There is now much greater recognition of infancy as a critical period for the development of the brain. This in turn has generated a debate, particularly in the USA, as to whether infants from birth should be 'hothoused', that is, subject to intensive external educational stimulation (Blakemore and Frith 2005). The environment has thus become a key element in brain development. For some the child's rapid biological growth is conditional on a highly stimulated 'hothouse' environment. Others are more cautious, arguing that minimum levels of stimulation are needed from parents and others to ensure that children's brains develop (Blakemore and Frith 2005). What this debate does demonstrate is the significance of research that takes account of neurological and sociological features of infancy.

These interests in the neurological dimensions of early development have converged into two educational and sociological focal points in the UK. This demonstrates some potential for interdisciplinary work. First the emphasis on stimulating brain growth in the early years connects with policy demands for more educational structure in the lives of children aged under five. Developments in early years' education in the UK have focused on the introduction of a curriculum for children from birth to five in England in 2006, the 'Early Years Foundation Stage' (EYFS) (Department of Children, Families and Schools 2006 Childcare Act 2006). This has generated a number of learning outcomes and assessment strategies. Thus in the updated version of EYFS there are seven 'areas of learning', three of which are critical, 'communication and language', 'physical development' and 'personal social and emotional development'. Four specific subject areas are also mentioned: 'literacy, mathematics, understanding the world and expressive arts and design' (Dept for Education 2012). There has been considerable criticism of the need for any curriculum for very young children (Eke, Butcher and Lee 2009). But what the EYFS does demonstrate is the way that education policy connects with research on early years' development.

Second, this research has been given added impetus from a growing body of evidence which emphasizes a significant developmental gap between children in poorer and more affluent families by the time they reach the age of three. The Millennium Cohort Study focuses on the early years with language and cognitive development markedly different for children from poorer backgrounds compared with their more affluent counterparts (CLS 2007). The researchers place particular emphasis on a child's 'school readiness' with children from families in poverty up to a year behind more affluent children by the time they reach three and thus less able to engage with the culture and expectations of the early years of primary school. Some years later, Gillies (2013) has argued that political support in the UK for investment in early years' education is premised on the notion that biological growth is determined by the nature of parenting in infancy. Thus problems that children have in the first years of schooling have been pathologized by leading politicians with parents and, in particular, mothers responsible for children's educational and developmental failings. While this is a reworking of a perennial generational 'cycle of poverty' theme, Gillies (2013) along with a number of others takes issue with this arguing for a multi-factorial and by implication multi-disciplinary approach that takes account of broader social structural factors. Thus sociological analysis of class differences between very young children emphasizes the way material, social and cultural factors interact with biological and cognitive aspects of children's 'growth'. For our purposes what is interesting here is the linkage between parental/maternal practice and the shaping of neurological growth. Gillies (2013) refers to a new UK government organization, the *Early Intervention Foundation*, with a remit to 'break the inter-generational cycles of dysfunction' (EIF 2013). The intention is that a range of bio-social research is drawn on in examining the link between infants' cognitive and emotional growth, the infant's genetic inheritance and routine parental practices. The critical focus here is on the link between biological growth, genetics and social practice.

In turning more generally to the Millennium Cohort Study (MCS), this multi-disciplinary research project tracks the development of 19,000 children born in the UK in 2000–1. The study follows these children into adulthood, exploring their cognitive, social, educational and economic wellbeing. A number of disparate areas related to the process of growing up are explored over time, among other things health, cognitive and language development, the quality of parenting and care and schooling and education. It is thus well placed to develop a more interdisciplinary approach to children and childhood. A wide range of data is collected from the children, their parents and siblings. Importantly, there are clear examples of attempts to evaluate and integrate biological and social and cultural factors. To take an example of the bio-social nexus from two of the many research focal points: the study involves biological surveys generating data from saliva samples that have been taken from children and parents (Calderwood and Rose 2013). Research has also been conducted on the possible early effects of ability groupings on the cohort as they progress through primary school (Campbell 2013). While the data from these two strands may or may not be correlated, the social aspects of children's lives in the classroom and the roles that adults play in shaping their educational wellbeing can be assessed against children's genetic codes from the saliva samples. This illustrates the breadth of this study in terms of the biological and social factors that constitute the process of children growing up. So we might be able to track genetic and socio-cultural factors that help to illuminate the various problems children might experience as they negotiate their schooling.

One other area where biological and socio-cultural work meets is analyses of children's bodies. If we turn briefly to the issue of embodiment: clear lines of difference were drawn in the early 1990s between developmental psychologists with a thoroughly embodied version of childhood and more radical versions of social constructionism where the child's body is reduced to a discursive representation with little material presence. Prendergast's (2000) research on young girls going through puberty offers an analysis that takes seriously the biological changes experienced in childhood and the social implications of these changes. She focuses on the relationship between the embodiment of childhood, particularly in young girls, and the processes through which they interpret and manage biological changes. Here we see the interface of biology and culture in terms of the ways that children shape their identities. What is particularly important here is that menstruation as an embodied experience has to be managed by girls very suddenly within a veil of ignorance and a context of secrecy. Girls' bodily changes are taboo subjects. Prendergast (2000) reports on the very limited knowledge available to young girls from family and the school. Thus far from being a natural process, girls often have to construct subtle and discreet strategies for managing these bodily changes – what are referred to as 'body maps'.

Children's and women's bodies have been prominent where the focus has been on the production of human life. It has been clear for many years that the 'natural' process of childbirth has been assisted by technology. Whether we are talking about amniocentesis, the application of pain relief or surgical intervention through a caesarean section, medical technology has altered the natural biological relationship between children and their parents. While there is clearly some debate around the benefits of technology in childbirth, arguably these initiatives have enhanced the role of human intervention in that mothers, parents more generally and professionals are able to make discretionary choices about the use of this technology (Wajcman 1991). In some respects notions of motherhood, parenthood and childbirth have conventionally been viewed as being natural, with children's relationship with parents assumed to be biologically based. In Chapter 4 I argued that the natural biological basis to family has been radically altered in the face of large numbers of children being brought up within reconstituted families where parenthood does not have a full genetic basis to it. Conception, reproduction and childbirth are heavily mediated by technology complicating the biological bond between parent and child. Thus, IVF challenges 'natural' processes of conception; genetic screening potentially alters the sex ratio at birth and gene therapy can manipulate what are commonly seen to be natural or genetic traits (Prout 2005). Medical science and technology compromise the idea that reproduction is basically about biological drives and instinctive urges. Any study of these processes brings technology, nature and culture together. Thus, analyses of bio-social nexus need to take account of the role of technology and social practices related to this technology.

Children's wellbeing

One area of global concern which has demanded a more multi-disciplinary response researching and working with children is children's wellbeing. The concept of children's wellbeing is a highly contested concept. Seedhouse (1995, p. 64) talks about it being subjective and 'essentially contested', the meaning of the concept largely based on the context within which it is being invoked and applied. It also acts as a broader frame within which more focused issues can be explored, such as poverty, mental health and educational attainment. It has taken on significance in more substantive terms with high-profile global reports on childhood focusing on wellbeing (UNICEF 2013, 2006a, b). In academic terms there is a journal devoted to the field, *Child Indicators Research* with a predominant focus on measuring wellbeing. Ben Arieh and Frones (2011, p. 463) refer to wellbeing as 'a desirable state of being happy, healthy or prosperous; but wellbeing is also related to the fulfilment of desires, to hedonism and the balance of pleasure and pain, to living conditions and so on'. But children's wellbeing as a concept has grown in importance as a consequence of the rights agenda. Drawing on the CRC Bradshaw and his colleagues provide a broad definition of wellbeing:

> Wellbeing can be defined as the realisation of children's rights and the fulfilment of the opportunity for every child to be all she or he can be in the light of a child's abilities, potential and skills. The degree to which this is achieved can be measured in terms of positive child outcomes, whereas negative outcomes and deprivation point to the neglect of children's rights. (Bradshaw et al. 2007, cited in Camfield et al. 2009, p. 66)

The CRC has become a reference point for the assessment of how well states, organizations and professionals underpin children's wellbeing. However, within a global context until fairly recently children's 'wellbeing' has had more negative connotations with research focusing on groups of the child population where wellbeing is absent or has been seriously compromised (Frydenberg et al. 2009). We could return to a negative deficit model of childhood discussed in Chapter 3, child labour. The international policy agenda on childhood is dominated by commitments to ending child labour, with a particular focus on the 'worst forms' of child labour. Child work is seen to compromise children's 'wellbeing' (see the review in Hesketh et al. 2006). As we argued there is broader international concern over the implications of this kind of participation for children's health, emotional wellbeing and schooling. In a review of the literature on the relationship between child labour and education commissioned by the ILO, the author concludes by stating that:

> child labour is increasingly being viewed as, above all, a human capital problem, measurable by its impacts

on education and health. The most recent decade of evidence corroborates this perspective and provides ample basis for taking action to reduce harmful impacts. (Dorman 2008, p. 47)

In some respects the heightening of negatives can be attributed to the dominance of bio-medical and psychological models of wellbeing (Boyden and de Berry 2004). In their analysis of the research field that underpins work on children and war, Boyden and de Berry (2004) argue that:

> (a)n almost exclusive focus on the intra-psychic function and impacts has certain adverse implications in terms of conceptualization of the issues. It reflects the tendency of psychological and medical assessments to ignore the wider societal destruction that is associated with most conflicts. In this way, studies have the effect of both pathologizing the survivors of conflict and individualizing a phenomenon that is profoundly political. (Boyden and de Berry 2004, p. xiv)

There is an emphasis here on treating the individual as affected by single events causing trauma with factors that can mitigate trauma, including the nature of social relations: the role of family peers and community and the influence of cultural practices being neglected. Children's wellbeing or its absence is compromised, as military conflict is argued to have universal negative outcomes on children's development. These effects are seen to be uniform in their impact on children: a developmental focus on children's biological and psychological wellbeing means that children of the same age and at roughly the same level of development are expected to experience military conflict in similar ways. Moreover, a focus on the medium and long-term effects means that developmental cohorts of children are expected to have similar problems as they move into adulthood. There are few analyses of the political, social and local contexts to this conflict which mediate the way children experience war. There is also little sense that these contexts provide opportunities for identifying children's agency in the way that they might negotiate conflict in their communities and regions. Others have argued that an emphasis on trauma is based on Western ideas that are less easily applicable in non-Western contexts (Bracken, Giller and Summerfield 1995). McAdam-Crisp (2006, p. 473) in her analysis of the effects of the genocide in Rwanda argues that the Rwandan language does not contain equivalents to the terms 'stress' and 'trauma'. Moreover, the concept and practice of counselling had little resonance in the affected communities despite being introduced by international aid organizations in the aftermath of the war.

More recent analyses have broadened the concept of harm to include economic, cultural and social variables as well as medical and psychological (Ben Arieh 2008). There are two key political moments here. First a broadened conception of wellbeing reflects the more holistic conception of childhood implicit within the CRC. As I argued in a previous chapter children now have rights that go beyond their physical and psychological survival, with children's civil, cultural and participatory rights now more central. Second, in the new millennium a range of reports has been published by UNICEF including the annual *State of the World's Children* with wellbeing a dominant theme. However, it is the UNICEF report card on children's wellbeing in the affluent North published in 2007 and 2013 that has generated most attention, with the UK and USA's lowly position within the rankings generating considerable publicity.[3] While there are no data on children's emotional wellbeing, the report card generates six dimensions of children's wellbeing, including physical, health and safety, behaviours and risks, educational, peer and family and subjective (UNICEF 2007). Thus we have a much broader conception of wellbeing here with the quality and quantity of children's social networks, and children's propensity for risky behaviour including under-age sex and the use of cannabis and alcohol included as well as more conventional measures of children's material and psychological wellbeing.

Children's subjective wellbeing

If we return to the discussion of children and war: children are viewed as relatively passive unformed bodies. From this vantage point there is little sense in which children themselves have the capacity to mediate the effects of war. However, broader analyses of wellbeing incorporate some conception of children having agency: as we discussed in Chapter 4, children are quite capable of effectively interacting with their environments and at the very least able to mediate some of the effects of war. With a growing attention towards children as agents, there is now some significance attached to children's own conceptions of wellbeing. One of the critical features of UNICEF's conception of wellbeing is children's own assessment of their wellbeing; this includes perceptions of their health, their schooling and their 'personal wellbeing'. In returning to the complex nature of wellbeing, a range of objective measures and indicators relating to children's physical and emotional development are now complemented and sometimes at odds with an interest in how children understand and feel about their lives. Children's subjective worlds have become a focal point, and subjective dimensions of wellbeing have become more prominent (Ben Arieh 2008). The CRC has become an important reference point for developing research approaches that incorporate children's voices (Camfield et al. 2009; Biggeri et al. 2006). Moreover, the globally contested nature of wellbeing and associated concepts such as resilience place a much higher premium on children themselves sharing their conceptions of wellbeing with others (McAdam-Crisp 2006). Biggeri et al. (2006) refer to a 'bottom-up' approach to researching children's wellbeing, with children initially surveyed and then interviewed about their understandings of their capabilities and wellbeing. Children were asked to reflect on a range of capabilities suggested by the researchers. Former child labourers were part of the sample. One interesting finding was the ambivalence expressed about children working as a feature of their capabilities. On the one hand, the children rejected the idea that work should be a central feature of children's lives. On the other hand, the children were aware that situations for many children globally were not ideal and they recognized the importance of children's work as a necessary feature of their families' domestic economy.

Camfield's (2012) work on Ethiopian children's conceptions of wellbeing is another good example. Taking into account location and gender the author discusses wellbeing in terms of what a 'good life' might mean to the children aged between eleven and thirteen. A vivid contrast is made between the rural children who were concerned with having enough food to live on and children from the urban research site who saw wellbeing as 'having a table full of a variety of food like a buffet' (Camfield 2012, pp. 208–9). Urban children mentioned material goods such as DVDs and cars. Rural children with more economic responsibilities were likely to emphasize better conditions for working such as irrigated land and boats for fishing. Education and good behaviour were ranked highly by all children but the former was more significant for the urban children than the rural children.

Multi-disciplinary research: global networks

There are now a number of research and organizational networks drawing on a range of disciplines exploring and tackling issues relating to children and wellbeing. The PsychoSocial Working Group was set up in 2000 by academics in Europe and the USA with the aim of providing intellectual support to government and aid agencies working with children in difficult global circumstances (PsychoSocial Working Group 2003). One of the focal points of the group is to explore the wellbeing of children in conflict situations. The group provides a conceptual framework for those working with children in a number of global regions consisting of three dimensions. First there is an emphasis on *human capacity* – the material and psychological wellbeing of children and their communities. Second reference is made to *social ecology*, which focuses on the quality and quantity of social relations and networks. Thirdly, there is an emphasis on *culture and values*, which locates children within specific regulatory and cultural contexts.

The Young Lives team based at the University of Oxford draws on these three areas in exploring the ways that children experience and negotiate poverty in countries in four regions of the world: India, Vietnam, Ethiopia, Peru. They take a longitudinal approach in tracking the lives of 12,000 children in these four regions over a fifteen-year period. The project has a number of distinctive features. First, it is multi-disciplinary, encompassing a range of social sciences and health and nutrition experts. The research is able to contextualize children's poverty from a number of different vantage points and explore the various strategies that enable children and their families to live with poverty. In this study nutritional experts extrapolate from nutritional measures of children's physical growth (assessments of the child's height for age) in the pre-school years to children's levels of cognitive ability in later school years. While causal links between children's physical development and later educational problems are fraught with difficulty, a more holistic approach to researching children's wellbeing will be able to identify the mechanisms within the family or the school that might mitigate these later difficulties. A more sociological approach is offered here. Parents' aspirations for their children may be driven by the child's physical stature. They can devote more resources to trying to improve the child's physical size in preparation for a life of manual labour. On the other hand, parents might try to ensure that the child improves his or her school performance as a means of maximizing the child's chances of gaining non-manual work (Hoddinott 2012).

Second, the Young Lives project adopts a mixed method strategy generating quantitative, demographic and economic data as well as more qualitative insights into children's lives from anthropology and sociology. The project thus generates multiple forms of data from a number of disciplinary vantage points. Third, it provides us with micro pictures of the daily routines of the children through the voices of the children themselves. These case studies offer us a more nuanced picture of how the children and their families mediate poverty. We have objective data on children's physical wellbeing and economic and health-related trends of families and communities. We also have research instruments generating data that are sensitized to more nuanced social and cultural factors.

Regional networks

At a regional level assessments have been made of children's wellbeing, drawing on a range of disciplinary vantage points. The African Child Policy Forum (ACPF) has commissioned a number of inquiries into a wide range of issues in relation to the wellbeing of African children. Thus a 2008 report focuses on the legal capacity of African states to protect children from being sexually exploited (ACPF 2008). More generally it has evaluated how child friendly African governments are according to a 'child friendly' index which ranked 52 states. Drawing on the CRC in terms of children's rights to provision, protection and participation they examined three dimensions of children's wellbeing which correspond to these rights: the extent to which a country has a legal framework for the protection of children; the capacity of a state to meet children's basic needs; and the existence of arrangements for children to participate in decisions that affect their wellbeing. The report draws on measures of these three dimensions in ranking African states with countries such as Mauritania, Kenya and South Africa categorized as 'most child friendly' Chad, Eritrea and the Central African Republic among those designated 'least child friendly' countries (ACPF 2008, p. 7). An updated version of this report was published in 2011 where there was a more economic focus. African states were assessed and ranked in terms of their economic capacity to provide for children's wellbeing. As the introduction clearly states, '(b)udgeting for children does not imply a separate budget for children. Rather, it involves examining the extent to which the needs of children are being addressed in the government's overall budget' (ACPF 2011, p. 1). An assessment is made of the funds allocated to children and how these funds are used in meeting the needs of children.

National research

In turning to national contexts we can look briefly at two countries' current attempts to assess their children's wellbeing from very different political and cultural contexts: Afghanistan and England.[4] Children's wellbeing was a focal point of the Children of Kabul report, which featured work undertaken with Afghan children and their families within the context of war (de Berry et al. 2003). The focus of this work was to identify with children and their parents the key features of a strategy for underwriting children's wellbeing. Importantly, the respondents argued that their wellbeing was not simply based on their physical survival of the current conflict. Thus children's emotional and spiritual wellbeing were seen as being just as important as their material survival. The quality of relationships that children have with their families, neighbours, faith leaders and peers are critical for children's abilities to cope with war. While material resources are needed, psycho-social approaches to intervention are recommended here. Thus support that helps to improve intergenerational relations as well as work within peer groups are seen as crucial to these Afghan children's wellbeing. Critically, these approaches build on the coping strategies that children have already developed.

In turning to our second example, England, there has lately been considerable emphasis on children's wellbeing. The publication of the Good Childhood Report in early 2009, based on a wide-ranging inquiry into the nature of modern British childhood, generated a national debate on the alleged crisis of childhood (Layard and Dunn 2009).[5] Again, as with the UNICEF report card, childhood and children's lives were explored in a more holistic way, with a broad range of indicators of children's lives drawn on in the discussion. While the concept of wellbeing is not explicitly referred to, among other things, the report discusses children's family life, their mental health, morality and social inequality.

Bradshaw's edited collection *The Well-Being of Children in the UK* is an attempt to provide a broader national picture of children's wellbeing in the UK. First published in 2001 there have been three subsequent updates since then, the latest published in 2011. A range of data are drawn on in setting out the wellbeing of children, incorporating the key areas found in the UNICEF report, as well as focusing on UK policy domains such as criminality, children in care and a demographic overview. One dimension neglected in the UNICEF report card, children's emotional wellbeing, is picked up by Bradshaw. There is little evidence to suggest a decline in levels of children's happiness despite UK children's lowly position within the UNICEF national rankings. In fact, if we draw on the British Youth Panel Survey (BYPS) children are happier in 2008 than they were in 1994 (Bradshaw and Keung 2011). The evidence is stronger for children's subjective wellbeing in relation to their schooling and their friendships. As with the Good Childhood inquiry (Layard and Dunn 2009), Bradshaw and Keung (2011) argue that the evidence on children with mental health problems has improved considerably with a consistent increase in problems from 1975 until 1999 tailing off from the turn of the century onwards. More specifically there has been a decrease in the number of younger children (aged 5–10) diagnosed with behavioural disorders from 3% in 1999 to 2% in 2004 and at the other end of the child 'age' spectrum there is a 14% decrease in the number of youth suicides between 2002 and 2008. Gender is significant here, with mental health being more of a problem for girls than boys, although the gap is narrowing, and poverty is a major factor underpinning the likelihood of children developing emotional and mental health problems.

Multi-disciplinary work: policy and practice

While debates on the disciplinary nature of work within the broad field of childhood studies presuppose a degree of contestation between different academic disciplines, Pain (2010) argues this excludes the voices of those from outside the academy. We have examined the position of children themselves in engaging with decisions relating to their wellbeing. We also need to explore the role that policy makers, organizations and professionals play. One of the critical features of childhood studies has been its potential to engage with policy makers and practitioners. In discussing the porous nature of disciplinary boundaries, particularly within childhood studies, it is also worth exploring parallel debates within the policy domain around the work done by different professional 'disciplines'. In some respects the increasing importance of childhood is reflected in a multi-layered public debate that crosses academic disciplines, policy realms and professional practice at local and global levels.

One particular version of children's wellbeing, children's welfare, has been a policy focus in England and Wales, where there has been an explosion of interest and activity in a range of welfare fields including child protection and education. Welfare here has revolved around two critical themes: the ongoing protection of children and the idea of children as investments in the future. We referred in the last chapter to how a series of high-profile cases of child abuse generated considerable public debate followed by major changes to the child protection system (Parton 2006). To take one example, in 1999 the abuse and subsequent death of an 8-year-old girl, Victoria Climbie, at the hands of her great aunt and her partner sparked major concerns over the extent to which various agencies were able to monitor the lives of children deemed at risk. This in turn instigated a major public review, the Laming Inquiry, which informed the revisions to the child protection system through the 2004 Children Act and to a lesser extent the 'every child matters' initiative. The state now plays an increasingly more regulatory role across a broad range of agencies. These trends have led to a much broader focus for providing children with structured holistic 'external' support (Parton 2011). 'Prevention' and 'risk' became buzz-words in the late 1990s as policy makers sought ways to support parents as early as possible and thus minimize difficulties they might encounter later on with their children. There was considerable investment by the Labour government in Sure Start children's centres in areas of socio-economic deprivation (Glass 1999). Further expansion in levels and forms of support for children took place in the early 2000s through the 'every child matters' initiative. This offered a more holistic conception of the child, with the state investing more broadly in children as future moral, social and economic beings. It also attempted to break down the state–family dichotomy by offering more networked support for children and their families. This involves social services, health, education and other agencies working more closely together with children and their families in order to strengthen systems of state support for children. Five areas of wellbeing were drawn on here: 'being healthy'; 'staying safe'; 'enjoying and achieving'; 'making a positive contribution'; and 'achieving economic wellbeing'. Each of these had a series of prescriptive targets and outcomes for practitioners from a range of different professions. Again, there are attempts being made to measure various aspects of children's wellbeing (Bradshaw 2011).

In the twenty-first century the political landscape has changed in England and Wales, with a coalition government and pressing economic pressures on state investment presaging a more circumspect social policy agenda. While Parton (2011) argues that social workers have been re-centred as primary agents within a system of child protection, there is still a sense in which concepts such as child wellbeing and welfare are only meaningfully applied where difficulties faced by children and their families can be tackled from a number of different vantage points. Moreover, the government has a commitment to wellbeing, or at least a non-monetary version of wellbeing, with the Prime Minister setting out his position a few years before coming to power

> It's time that we admitted that there is more to life than money, and it's time that we focused not just on GDP but GWB General Well Being. It's about the beauty of our surroundings, quality of our culture, and above all the strength of our relationships. (David Cameron 2006, cited in Bradshaw 2011, p. 91)

While the 'every child matters' initiative was broad in focus there was nevertheless a limited emphasis on children's emotional wellbeing. The educational policy agenda rectified this to some extent in offering a number of disparate initiatives focusing on children's socio-emotional wellbeing. The Social and Emotional Aspect of Learning (SEAL) was set up to improve children's emotional capacity to learn (DCSF 2007). The National Healthy Schools Programme was set up jointly by the then Department for Education and Science and the Department of Health, which had an important commitment to 'emotional health and wellbeing' within schools. The Peer Mentoring Pilot scheme was initiated in 2007 to explore the effectiveness of peer support networks in school and counter the rising problem of bullying in school, a problem that has particularly damaging consequences for young people's emotional and social wellbeing. In broad policy and practice terms in England there is a more networked approach to supporting children which involves exploring children and childhood from a number of different vantage points.

The 'every child matters' initiative reinforced this earlier holistic approach to social exclusion. If we take the example of an edition of *Community Care*, a professional journal available nationally for UK social workers, there is advice on

'How to work in Multi-Disciplinary Teams' (2005). The article refers to 'ways of creating resilient multi-professional teams'. More specifically there are five sets of ideas:

- Defining the roles and boundaries of team members and thus generating greater awareness of disciplinary differences.
- Being aware of 'power dynamics', and thus taking more care not to assert one disciplinary approach over another.
- Being aware that different disciplines have different perspectives on clients; finding ways of minimizing the extent to which clients can exploit these differences.
- Exploring ways in which decision making can be distributed across the team. 'Any action to be taken should be a shared vision owned by all team members.'
- Consider incorporating the participation of 'service users', children and their families as part of a multi-disciplinary team.

In the earlier discussion in the chapter on multi-disciplinarity I referred to the way that biological and sociological research reinforced demands for a more structured educational approach to pre-schoolers. The Early Years Foundation Stage curriculum (EYFS) exemplifies this approach. A revised version of this curriculum expands the work for early years' teachers. Teachers have more explicit 'welfare requirements' (DfE 2012). While the safeguarding of children was a major responsibility of all professionals working with children in the post 'every child matters' era, there is now more explicit reference to early years' teachers having a greater awareness of child protection matters. Two of the welfare requirements are worth mentioning:

> *Child protection*: the revised EYFS includes examples of adults' behaviour which might be signs of abuse and neglect. If they become aware of any such signs, staff should respond appropriately in order to safeguard children.

> *Suitable people*: the requirements for providers to check the suitability of managers have been simplified. From September 2012, providers will be responsible for obtaining criminal record disclosures on managers. Currently, Ofsted obtain these disclosures.
>
> (DfE 2012)

A multi-agency approach has been a feature of child-related policy in England since the late 1990s. While wellbeing here has been constructed as an issue involving the social, educational and material aspects of childhood, the application of multi-disciplinary principles has proved much more difficult to apply in practice. Various authors have identified professional, cultural and practical barriers to professionals from disparate backgrounds working together (Milbourne, Macrae and Maguire 2003; Bagley, Ackerley and Rattray 2004). Milbourne et al. (2003) analysed the UK Labour government's commitment to tackling social exclusion through the opening up of Sure Start centres and the introduction of Education Action Zones and Health Action Zones. While Sure Start focused on trying to engage with hard to reach families with pre-school children, the Education and Health Action Zones targeted areas where there were inequalities in access to health care and levels of educational attainment. The empirical focus was an initiative based in a primary school in one such Educational and Health Action Zone, where social workers, health professionals and educationalists were working together to combat high rates of primary school exclusion. The policy and practice emphasis was on 'multi-agency partnerships'. However, there were major problems in developing and maintaining these partnerships. In practical and political terms the lack of time afforded the participants in putting the 'partnership' together and the pressure on agencies to deliver outcomes from the project made it difficult for the different agencies to form viable working relationships. Moreover, ongoing professional tensions were evident in terms of the status, expertise and knowledge base of the educationalists, the health professionals and the case workers. Milbourne and her colleagues (2003) nicely illustrate much broader tensions between disciplines and subject areas working together. While the authors illustrate the difficulties of carrying through explicit policy commitments to collaborative working on short-term outcomes oriented and poorly resourced initiatives at the local level, they also identify more general issues relating to tensions emerging from within a multi-agency team.

One particular issue was leadership of a multi-disciplinary team: in this instance there was no lead agency which had implications for the direction and continuous focus of the project. As one participant stated:

> I mean it raises questions about whether one agency should have been given overall control and whether the two other agencies would give that permission and whether that would be right for all contexts in multi-agency work. If only one agency had a management responsibility, there would be some sense of holding responsibility and determinant; as it is, the whole thing becomes more ambiguous and people aren't sure what direction to pull in. (Milbourne et al. 2003, p. 26)

Ambiguity here is pitched at the level of confusion and frag-mentation. However, any attempt at providing a more focused and coherent approach generates further ambiguity. A more focused approach driven by a single agency is seen here as a precondition of success. At the same time getting to a position where other agencies are committed to one agency having overall control risks generating tensions between the agencies with and without control. An associated issue is the relative status of a professional's qualifications. As one professional in Milbourne et al.'s study noted: '(W)ithin the sort of multi-agency set up, there are ideas around qualifications, and who's got the best qualifications. There's quite a lot of snob-bery around, you know, what your qualification is, which discipline you belong to' (op. cit.).

There were also issues about how the application of disci-plinary knowledge by each professional sometimes brought them into conflict. One particular issue was the difficulty reconciling the individualistic approach of the educational psychologist with the relational 'family centred' approach of the social worker. This tension was picked up by the head teacher from the school that housed the project.

> I felt that when they came in, the team would work in the school but, in fact, it was just the one, and her background was psychology. I think it's a shame actually, but well I just feel that for some children perhaps they needed more, as much social work as they needed psychology. (ibid. p. 29)

More broadly, the authors refer to difficulties gaining any consensus among the different professionals over the key aims of the project and the nature of multi-agency working. We come back to the difficulties of developing an interdisciplinary approach: an agreement among the various disciplines as to the precise nature of the problem being tackled. There are parallels between the inter-agency and interdisciplinary approaches at professional and academic levels respectively. Issues of ontology, knowledge and status underpin and compromise the ability of researchers from different disciplines to work effectively on a range of child-related research problems. Just as agencies with the best intentions of improving the life chances of their young clients can sometimes work against each other, so the pursuit of knowledge within the field of children and childhood can be compromised by 'paradigmatic' differences.

It is unclear as to the precise relationship between an expanded childhood studies incorporating a diversity of disciplinary fields and a policy aspiration for more networked support across a range of agencies for children and their families. However, there may be resonances or what Weber (1992) calls 'elective affinities' between the two realms of child-related action. At the very least the political and professional commitment to multi-agency working with children in England and Wales in some respects mirrors calls for much closer cross-disciplinary work within childhood studies. There is certainly the potential for a dialogical relationship between the academic and political and professional spheres. There has been a major expansion in theorizing and empirical work within the fields of children and childhood. Much of this work has taken place in northern Europe but there are developing pockets of research activity within North America, Australasia and many other regions within the Southern hemisphere. One area where dialogue between the socio-political and social scientific spheres of activity has taken place is children's participation. There is a much broader and well-established international discourse on participation here: for example, the Participatory Rural Appraisal approach (PRA) has become a standard approach to international development within the South. Working from Paolo Freire's notion of community empowerment, PRA emphasizes the role of local communities working alongside international aid organizations in developing initiatives to improve the wellbeing of populations (Chambers 1994). Drawing on this approach there is also an expectation now within child-related fields on international policy and practice that children as well as adults are key actors in this development. In parallel there is also a well-established body of theoretical and empirical work on children's participation within the international field (Percy-Smith and Thomas 2010). There is an important convergence between these two spheres of work with the CRC providing an ever-present backdrop to policy makers, practitioners and academics within the field. There are also some clear examples of policy borrowing from the academy. Take, for example, UNICEF's citing of Hart's work referred to in Chapter 3. Moreover, researchers within the field of children's participation have taken a much more explicitly political role in promoting children's rights, particularly children's rights to participate. Most of the contributions in Percy-Smith and Thomas' (2010) collection of papers on participatory contexts and initiatives in a wide range of international settings are explicitly advocating more democratic relations between children and adults.

Conclusion

A renewed interest in the concept of childhood and the lives of children has generated a complex array of disciplinary focal points and professional practices. In some cases these have been disciplinary claims on the nature of childhood and the wellbeing of the children. These claims have brought psychology into conflict with sociology. Developmental assumptions are questioned as sociologists discover practices in which children routinely belie their developmental age and position. Furthermore, a more global focus has made it much more difficult for the developmental frame to have sufficient authoritative resonance in a number of disparate cultural contexts. In Foucauldian terms development as a 'regime of truth' is challenged. The new childhood studies has often been seen as an epistemological break, with the old biological assumptions about childhood giving way to more social and cultural approaches that stress the construction of childhood.

However, revisions of the field have argued that a bio-social dualism has been overstated. Given the higher political, professional and academic visibility of children as global investments and agents, there is arguably much more commitment to childhood as a bio-social nexus. That is, a broader holistic conception of childhood has generated attempts to capture the 'breadth' and complexity of children's lives from a number of different vantage points. A bio-social nexus has the potential to form a nucleus for more multi-disciplinary approaches to researching and working with children. There are possibilities in generating an increase in dialogue and debate between a number of disciplines, in particular, a means of bringing sociological and psychological disciplines together. Children's wellbeing has become a familiar global frame of reference with governments being more accountable for their commitment to underwrite children's material, psychological and social integrity.[6] At the same time it has become an important reference point for researching children's lives in a number of disparate cultural and political contexts. Wellbeing has thus become a framework within which multi-disciplinary research on children's lives takes place.

The limits of an interdisciplinary approach to some extent mirror the limits of a modernist project to protect and regulate children carefully as future investments. While a multi-disciplinary approach implies different disciplines working together, sometimes in parallel, a postmodernist framework would challenge the idea of a fully integrated approach to childhood, not least because there is no consensus over the meaning of childhood or any proposed agenda for improving children's wellbeing. Despite the lack of consensus among disciplines, what a postmodernist approach does promise are opportunities for voices to be heard from outside the academy. Firstly, children themselves are often featured in wellbeing research. Secondly, the politicizing of childhood has generated multi-agency spaces within which professionals are expected to work more closely together in assessing risk, improving outcomes and in general protecting children as future investments. Thus while there is some doubt as to whether an interdisciplinary is possible within childhood studies there is some evidence of a polyvocal approach to children and childhood.

Conclusion: Relocating Children and Childhood

In this book I focused on agency, globalization and generation as contested concepts within childhood studies. Within the social sciences the former two have been the subject of considerable debate. While agency has a paradigmatic status within childhood studies, work within the field has questioned this status opening up the term to more rigorous conceptual interrogation (Oswell 2013; Valentine 2011). Similarly, globalization has become an overused term, with a conflicting conceptual and epistemological status as both a 'cause' and 'effect' of major macro changes (Prout 2005). At the same time its loose, fluid and porous nature has been noted by a number of scholars (Scholte 2005). In this book I have applied globalization as a useful shorthand for wide-scale political, economic and cultural changes that both expand and limit the possibilities for children and offer a sharper frame within which to critically analyse the conceptualizing of childhood. The third theme of the book, generation, is a relatively recent bundle of ideas. With the notable exception of Mannheim, the concept of generation has little significant application outside of childhood studies, and arguably still plays a minor role within the dominant discipline of sociology within childhood studies (Alanen 2009). Nevertheless, despite its marginal 'novelty' status it offers something new within the broader academy in its insistence that children's generational status and location can be drawn on in analysing various problems and opportunities for children.

In bringing the three themes of the book together, what I am trying to do is to relocate children and childhood within broader social, political and academic contexts. Two key trends dominate the public and political realms, social change and its effects on children and childhood, and intermittent and chronic problems affecting children, with the latter often eclipsing the former within narratives on childhood. Within contemporary narratives there is still a recourse to modernist conceptions of childhood. Global problems of civil war, poverty, the HIV/AIDS pandemic and exploitation dispro- portionately affect children and generate concerns over the exposure of children to physical, emotional and moral risk. Moreover, there are also major challenges to the integrity of family, community and welfare infrastructures and regulatory systems within which children are located. Issues of depend- ence, protection and futurity dominate with overriding con- cerns among policy makers, professionals and academics to narrow the gap between 'deficit' and 'normal' childhoods at national and global levels. Regulatory systems are now con- structed to minimize the risk to children's wellbeing. At the same time there have also been substantial changes to the legal, political and social status of children. These changes to children's lives have become focal points for analyses within childhood studies.

There is little doubt that there is a much stronger emphasis within these analyses on new roles, positions and spaces for children and childhood. While public and political commentary is at best ambiguous in defining these positions for children, childhood studies has tended to take a more sanguine line embracing and expanding social repertoires and networks within which children are positioned. Three positions stand out:

• *Structural*: children here have become a constituent feature of the social structure. Children are no longer located on the periphery of the social world as social apprentices; they are of the social world occupying generational positions. This social structural approach to children and childhood has important political ramifications with the rise of the rights-bearing child connecting with children's struc- tural position as a means of understanding and theorizing children as a collective; a subordinated group or social minority. Moreover, a structural approach explores the interplay between children as agents and their location as subordinates with a generational structure.

- *Interstitial*: changes to family structures and welfare systems, as well as major challenges to communities as a consequence of civil war, disease and poverty, have relocated children in more interstitial positions as participants and mediators in between conventional public and private realms and between more complex networks of institutions, political structures and localized economic markets. In the book I have illustrated the range of interstitial roles that children as social agents play from weaker forms in education systems through to more prominent roles mediating between transnational families and local communities and political structures.

- *Productive*: in their families and communities, in effect, in a much broader range of social contexts, children create, imagine and generate resources in material and virtual terms. Children's roles as carers, income providers, social knowledge producers extend and complicate their more conventional modernist positions as dependants, emotional subjects and human capital future class and gender bearers. Moreover, children's productive roles are particularly prominent in processes of identity formation. In fluid and global contexts children are adept at drawing on a range of resources in surprising and unpredictable ways in developing their own senses of self.

I have argued that these roles are predominantly social in character, which reflects the general rise in the social domain within childhood studies. First, the social constructionist approach rivals, if not usurps, the position of developmental psychology as the dominant narrative within the broader study of childhood. Second, children's agency which emerged as a possibility from social constructionism has now achieved paradigmatic status within childhood studies. Later revisions of children's agency have focused on its social and relational nature. Third, child–adult relations are located within broader generational structures, which introduce a generational dimension to broader social structures. Children and adults helping to refine the categories of 'child' and 'adult' through ongoing social interactions between them. Fourth, the idea of a generational order has important political ramifications. Children are now more likely to be viewed as a social class by virtue of social rather than individual or psychological criteria.

The reframing of agency

In terms of the framing of children's agency I have outlined the move from a modernist childhood through to a more postmodern conception, with the recognition of agency one of the critical differences between the two models. In this book I have characterized a postmodernist conception of childhood in terms of children's participation, in relation to their use of technology and in terms of the possibilities for identity formation. A key theme running through the book is the legitimacy of agency. There is a range of perspectives from within childhood studies from the individualist to the relational; from the adult free to the inter-generational. However, within the broader society at national and global levels agency is heavily circumscribed; agency has a more discursive focus. A dominant postmodern conception of childhood emphasizes adult-regulated discursive models of participation. I have argued that this has the effect of both misrecognizing and marginalizing other more material forms of agency. What I have tried to do in this book is explore the different and multiple vantage points for understanding agency which underpin more diverse forms of childhood. Moreover, this range of perspectives has been discussed in terms of different realms of 'childhood', firstly within childhood studies through the multi-disciplinary shaping of agency; secondly, in terms of children's own conceptions of agency; and thirdly, through political, professional and institutional applications of agency.

Children as a global constituency

The book has also identified children as a global constituency with much higher levels of public and political levels of visibility. International agencies, supra-national organizations like the UN and a powerful global network of media have defined children as a separate sector of the global population. Children at this level are viewed as rights bearers and are much more intensively governed, particularly in Western affluent countries. This has generated conflicting conceptions inviting quite different responses from national governments and agencies. On the one hand, children are a social minority group, a globally disadvantaged group as a result of their subordinate position within the generational hierarchy. In these terms we can reconceptualize their inequality, their poverty and their maltreatment as an immanent feature of their childhood status. In Chapter 5 I applied a generational approach to the problem of child abuse. Thus while particular groups of children are more likely to be maltreated than others, children's relative lack of power and their lowly subordinate status, particularly within school, opens children up to the risk of maltreatment. On the other hand, children are now more likely to be recognized as a constituent element of change in that global shifts in information and communication technologies and commitments to children's voices have benefited children, their families and communities and shifted the focus towards children as participants and social agents.

In rethinking children's status as participants in global terms we have tackled issues of inequality and exploitation from a number of different angles. While issues of responsibility, work and civil war undoubtedly compromise children's life chances and increase inequalities between different groups of children, they also offer opportunities for identifying and sometimes reassessing children's roles within their families and communities. The analyses of child labourers and young carers in Chapter 4 and the concept of wellbeing in Chapter 5 shifted the focus away from deficit models of childhood and emphases on children's status as victims and dependants. Issues of interdependence are critical here: children's varied roles and responsibilities emerge out of ongoing relations that children have with family members, other adults and their peers. In returning to Mayall's (2002) conceptions of generation focusing on children's positions within the social structure, they have broader relations with ideas and practices that tie children and adults together. Children and adults draw on this repertoire of resources at a more local level in the way that they negotiate their relationships with friends, peers and families.

Childhood studies

Given the rise of children's agency and the growing global awareness of children, what can we say about trends within childhood studies? In the book I have identified a range of global issues affecting children and our conceptualizations of childhood. In turn this has made greater demands on researchers to draw on more holistic frameworks in tackling these issues. Among a range of current trends globalization picks up on the growing complexity of children's lives which includes demands from children themselves for more access to and control of agendas. There are thus social and political pressures on researchers to work across a range of theoretical frameworks and disciplines in exploring challenges, problems and relations experienced by children. In Chapter 5 we set out the conceptual grounds for a more child-specific approach to analysing children's positions within the social structure. At the same time there are also grounds for thinking that a generational approach probably works best when in conjunction with more conventional analytical frameworks. This generates a more nuanced understanding of children's lives across social, cultural and age-related spectrums. At a disciplinary level in Chapter 6 we explored the potential and limitations of an interdisciplinary approach to studying children and childhood. The current state of play here is unclear, with more integrated empirical work encountering resistance at the levels of principle and practice. Nevertheless, there is a move towards a bio-social nexus, with work on the psychological and social wellbeing of children offering possibilities for interdisciplinary work. Thus, the earlier impetus to relegate developmentalism to a marginal position within childhood studies and the concomitant rise of the social domain is largely being superseded by a rapprochement between the social and biological fields.

It is also clear that childhood incorporates a more poly-vocal debate across a range of different realms with policy makers playing an increasingly more prominent role in estab-lishing research agendas. The national and global visibility of children potentially brings the political realm closer to the academy, generating opportunities to work on behalf of chil-dren in improving their conditions, experiences and life chances. At the same time the propinquity of research, policy and practice generates conflicts between the academic com-mitment to agency, voice and political commitments to tight-ening regulatory frameworks within which children are located. This expansive network of 'childhood' interests and commitments is further extended if we incorporate the voices and commitments of children. The final point brings us back to the children themselves. While children still play a periph-eral role in these debates and have limited agenda-setting powers, this discourse stretches across a messy patchwork of theorizing, research, policy and practice at local, national and global levels. Children insinuate themselves in and through these regulations, ideas, practices and relationships as some-times muted, but more often than not, vocal social agents.

Notes

1 Conceptualizing Agency

1 Other theorists of agency conflate 'action' and 'agency'. See Giddens (1984).
2 We will have more to say about this in the discussion of the paradox of agency later in the chapter.
3 McAdam-Crisp (2006), in her analysis of children's roles in the Rwandan Genocide in 1994, notes that almost 3,000 children were imprisoned for their involvement in the genocide.

2 The Recognition and Distribution of Children's Agency

1 Some crisis theorists have argued that, logically, if childhood is disappearing so must adulthood. See Postman (1995).
2 The issue of sexting has come to the attention of the criminal justice system in England and Wales with The Child Exploitation and On-line Protection Centre (CEOP) recently publishing guidelines (Association of Chief Police Officers of England, Wales and Northern Ireland (n.d.).
3 Parents here were members of the Mothers' Union, a long-standing Christian charity that supports family life.
4 Around 90% of lone parents are mothers.

3 Childhood, Globalization and Global Standards

1 While there is no consensus on the use of terms such as the South, the developing world, or less affluent regions when talking about non-Western contexts, I will refer to Southern contexts.
2 Left behind American Children in China, *Offbeat China*, 6 December 2012; China's left behind children: an embarrassing side-effect of rapid development, *The China Diaries*, 16 January 2013.
3 It is estimated that the 2010 figures will show that this MDG has been reached (United Nations 2012).
4 ILO Convention 138 was passed in 1973 defining child labourers as those below the age of fifteen.
5 The 1998 Rome Statute defines the recruitment of children into the army as a war crime.

4 Childhoods: Diversity and Hybridity

1 While the focus of this analysis is the contraction of HIV/ AIDS by parents, we need to acknowledge that the pandemic has also had a direct impact on children themselves with 390,000 children under the age of fifteen infected by HIV/AIDS worldwide (UNICEF 2011).
2 While there is no global definition of what constitutes an orphan, I use the UN's definition: orphans are children who lose at least one parent. See Mavise (2011).
3 Some of these factors are related more generally to children forming child-headed households, particularly the last two points.

5 Childhood and Generation

1 Although this can be a substantial and expanding proportion of the life cycle.
2 Although there is a less well established notion of 'elder abuse'. See Pinsker et al. (2010); Biggs et al. (2009).
3 The difficulties in identifying trends in child abuse can itself be partly explained by the same cultural and social factors that help to explain abuse.
4 See the US federal law Title 18 of the United States Code, 2422 Coercion and Entitlement and Sexual Offences Act 2003 in the UK.

5 See, for example, Christensen and Mikkelsen's (2011) work on Danish girls' collective strategies for creating their own spaces away from adult surveillance.

6   Childhood, Wellbeing and Multi-Disciplinarity

1 See, for example, issue 2 (2012) Children as Knowledge Producers.
2 If anything Piaget's insistence of children's developing capacities to master their environments suggests a particular conception of competence.
3 The most recent version of this report refers to Britain's improved ranking (UNICEF 2013).
4 We can also find versions of these discussions in other global contexts. See Hur and Testerman's (2012) work on wellbeing in North Carolina, USA, and Saith and Wazir (2010) with respect to India.
5 Part of this debate was discussed in Chapter 2 in relation to children's 'premature sexualization'.
6 Interestingly, Saith and Wazir (2010) refer to the dominance of economic conceptions of wellbeing in India. They compare this situation with more affluent countries where there is a much broader multi-factoral conception of children's wellbeing.

References

Abebe, T. (2007) Changing livelihoods, changing childhoods: patterns of children's work in rural Ethiopia, *Children's Geographies*, 5 (1–2): 77–93.

Abi-Rached, J. and Rose, N. (2010) The birth of the neuromolecular gaze, *History of Human Sciences*, 23 (1): 11–36.

African Child Policy Forum (ACPF) (2011) *The African Report on Child Wellbeing: Budgeting for Children*, Addis Ababa: The African Child Policy Forum.

— (2008) *Sexual Exploitation of Children in Africa: Legal Frameworks and Law Enforcement*, http://www.unicef.org/wcaro/Sexual_l_Exploitation_paper_World_Congress_Final__2_.pdf

Ahn, J. (2010) 'I'm not scared of anything': emotion as social power in children's worlds, *Childhood*, 17 (1): 94–112.

Aitken S., Lund, R. and Kjorholt, A. (eds) (2009) *Global Childhoods, Globalisation, Development and Young People*, London: Routledge.

Alanen, L. (2012) Disciplinarity, interdisciplinarity and childhood studies, *Childhood*, 19 (4): 419–22.

— (2009) Generational order, in J. Qvortrup, W. Corsaro and M.-S. Honig (eds) *The Palgrave Handbook of Childhood Studies*, Basingstoke: Palgrave.

Alderson, P. (2008) *Young Children's Rights, Exploring Beliefs, Principles and Practice*, 2nd edn, London: Jessica Kingsley.

— (1994) Researching children's rights to integrity, in B. Mayall (ed.) *Children's Childhoods Observed and Experienced*, London: Falmer.

American Psychological Association (2007) *Sexualization of Girls: Executive Summary*, http://www.apa.org/pi/women/programs/girls/report.aspx

Amuedo-Dorantes, C. and Pozo, A. S. (2010) *Accounting for Remittance and Migration Effects on Children's Schooling*, Barcelona:

Institute for Economic Analysis http://www.insidenet.org/wp-content/files_flutter/1267018567Inside_15.pdf

Ansel, N. and van Blerk, L. (2007) Doing and belonging: towards a representational account of young migrant workers in Lesotho and Malawi, in R. Panelli, S. Punch and E. Robson (eds) *Global Perspectives on Rural Childhood and Youth*, London: Routledge.

Archer, M. (2000) *Being Human: The Problem of Agency*, Cambridge: Cambridge University Press.

Arendt, H. (1959) *The Human Condition*, Chicago: University of Chicago Press.

Ariès, P. (1961) *Centuries of Childhood*, Harmondsworth: Penguin.

Arild Vis, S. and Thomas, N. (2009) Beyond talking: children's participation in Norwegian care and protection cases, *European Journal of Social Work*, 12 (2): 155–68.

Association of Chief Police Officers of England, Wales and Northern Ireland (ACPO) (n.d.) *ACPO CPAI Lead's Position on Young People Who Post Self-Taken Indecent Images*. http://www.ceop.police.uk/Documents/ceopdocs/externaldocs/ACPO_Lead_position_on_Self_Taken_Images.pdf

Avert (n.d.) *Children Orphaned by HIV and AIDS* http://www.avert.org/aids-orphans.htm#to

Baginsky, M. and Hannam, D. (1999) *School Councils: The views of students and teachers*, London: National Society for the Prevention of Cruelty to Children.

Bagley, C., Ackerley, C. and Rattray, J. (2004) Social exclusion, Sure Start and organisation social capital: evaluating inter-agency working in an education and health programme, *Journal of Education Policy*, 19 (5): 595–607.

Ball, S. (2003) *Class Strategies and the Education Market: The Middle Classes and Social Advantage*, London: Routledge Falmer.

Banks, C. (2007) The discourse of children's rights in Bangladesh: international norms and local definitions, *International Journal of Children's Rights*, 15 (3 and 4): 391–414.

Barber, T. (2007) Young people and civic participation: a conceptual review, *Youth and Policy* (96) Summer: 19–39.

Barker, J. (2003) Passengers or political actors? Children's involvement in transport policy and the micro-political geographies of the family, *Space and Polity*, 7 (2): 131–51.

Barrett, B. (2012) Is interdisciplinarity old news? A disciplined consideration of inter-disciplinarity, *British Journal of Sociology of Education*, 33 (1): 97–114.

Beck, U. and Beck-Gernsheim, E. (1995) *The Normal Chaos of Love*, Cambridge: Polity.

Ben-Arieh, A. (2008) The child indicators movement: past, present and future, *Child Indicators Research*, 1: 3–16.

Ben Arieh, A. and Frones, I. (2011) Taxonomy for child well-being indicators: a framework for the analysis of the well-being of children, *Childhood*, 18 (4): 460–76.

Bendle, M. (2002) The crisis of 'identity' in high modernity, *British Journal of Sociology*, 53 (1): 1–18.

Berman, E. (2011) The irony of immaturity: K'iche' children as mediators and buffers in adult social interactions, *Childhood*, 18 (2): 274–88.

Bernstein, B. (1971) *Class Codes and Control*, vol. 1, London: Paladin.

Bethke Elshtain, J. (1996) Commentary: political children, *Childhood*, 3 (1): 11–28.

Beveridge, S. (2004) Pupil participation and the home–school relationship, *European Journal of Special Needs Education*, 19 (1): 3–16.

Biao, X. (2007) How far are the left-behind left behind? A preliminary study in rural China, *Population, Space and Place*, 13 (3): 179–91.

Biggeri, M., Libanora, R., Mariani, S. and Menchini, L. (2006) Children conceptualising their capabilities: Results of a survey conducted during the First World Congress on Child Labour, *Journal of Human Development*, 7 (1): 59–83.

Biggs, S., Manthorpe, J., Tinker, A., Doyle, M. and Erens, B. (2009) Mistreatment of older people in the United Kingdom: findings from the first national prevalence study, *Journal of Elder Abuse and Neglect*, 21: 1–14.

Birnbaum, R. and Saini, M. (2013) A scoping review of qualitative studies about children experiencing parental separation, *Childhood*, 20 (2): 260–82.

Bissell, S. (2003) The social construction of childhood: a perspective from Bangladesh, in N. Kabeer, G. Nambissan and R. Subrahmanian (eds) *Child Labour and the Right to Education in South Asia*, London: Sage.

Bjerke, H. (2011) 'It's the way they do it': expressions of agency in child–adult relations at home and at school, *Children and Society*, 25 (2): 93–103.

Bjorkland, A., Ginther, D. and Sundstrom, M. (2007) Family structure and child outcomes in the USA and Sweden, *Journal of Population Economics*, 20 (1): 183–201.

Blagborough, J. (2008) Child domestic labour: a modern form of slavery, *Children and Society*, 22 (3): 179–90.

Blakemore, S. and Frith, U. (2005) *The Learning Brain Lessons for Education*, Oxford: Blackwell.

Bluebond-Langner, M. (1994) A child's view of death, *Current Paediatrics*, 4 (4): 253–7.

Bluebond-Langner, M. and Korbin, J. (2007) Challenges and opportunities in the anthropology of childhoods: an introduction to 'children, childhoods, and childhood studies', *American Anthropologist*, 109 (2): 241–6.

Bond, E. (2010) Managing mobile relationships: children's perceptions of the impact of the mobile phone on relationships in their everyday lives, *Childhood*, 17 (4): 514–29.

Bottcher, L. (2009) The dialectic relations between neurobiological constraints and activity in child development, in M. Fleer, M. Hedegaard and J. Tudge (eds) *Childhood Studies and the Impact of Globalisation: Practices at Global and Local Levels*, London: Routledge, pp. 108–22.

Bourdieu, P. and Wacquant, L. (1992) *An Invitation to Reflexive Sociology*, Cambridge: Polity.

Bourdillon, M. (2006) Children and work: a review of current literature and debates, *Development and Change*, 37 (6): 1201–26.

Boyden, J. (1997) Childhood and policy makers: a comparative perspective on the globalization of childhood, in James and Prout (eds) *Constructing and Reconstructing Childhood*, Basingstoke: Falmer, pp. 190–229.

Boyden, J. and de Berry, J. (2004) Introduction, in J. Boyden and J. de Berry (eds) *Children and Youth on the Front Line: Ethnography Conflict and Displacement*, New York: Berghahn Books.

Bracken, P., Giller, J. E. and Summerfield, D. (1995) Psychological responses to war and atrocity: the limitations of current concepts, *Social Science and Medicine*, 40 (8): 1073–82.

Bradshaw, J. (2011) Introduction, in J. Bradshaw (ed.) *The Well-Being of Children in the UK*, London: *Save the Children*, UK.

Bradshaw, J. and Keung, A. (2011) Subjective wellbeing and mental health, in J. Bradshaw (ed.) *The Well-Being of Children in the UK*, London: Save the Children, UK.

Bragg, S. (2012) Dockside tarts and modesty boards: a review of recent policy on sexualisation, *Children and Society*, 26 (5): 406–14.

Brake, M. (1995) *Comparative Youth Culture: The Sociology of Youth Cultures and Youth Sub-cultures*, London: Routledge.

Bromley, R. and Mackie, P. (2009) Child experiences as street traders in Peru: contributing to a reappraisal of working children, *Children's Geographies*, 7 (2): 141–58.

Brown, G. and Pickerill, J. (2009) Space for emotion in the spaces of activism, *Emotion, Space and Society*, 2 (1): 24–35.

Buckingham, D. (2000) *After the Death of Childhood: Growing up in the Electronic Media*, Cambridge: Polity.

Buckingham, D. and Bragg, S. (2004) *Young People, Sex and the Media: the Facts of Life?* Basingstoke: Palgrave.

Buckingham, D. and de Block, L. (2007) *Global Children, Global Media*, Basingstoke: Palgrave.

Bundy, C. (1987) Street sociology and pavement politics: aspects of youth and student resistance in Cape Town, *Journal of Southern African Studies*, 13 (3): 303–30.

Bunting, L., Webb, M. and Healey, J. (2010) In two minds? Parental attitudes toward physical punishment in the UK, *Children and Society*, 24 (5): 359–70.

Burman, E. (2007) *Deconstructing Developmental Psychology*, 2nd edn, London: Routledge.

Burr, R. (2004) Children's rights: international policy and lived practice, in M. J. Kehily (ed) *An Introduction to Childhood Studies*, Buckingham: Open University.

Butler, U. M. (2009) Freedom, revolt and 'citizenship': Three pillars of identity for youngsters living on the streets of Rio de Janeiro, *Childhood*, 16 (1): 11–29.

Calderwood, L. and Rose, N. (2013) Collecting saliva samples for DNA extraction from children and parents: *Evidence from the UK Millennium Cohort Study*, CLS Working Papers 2013/3, London: Centre for Longitudinal Studies.

Camfield, L. (2012) Pen, book, soap, good food and encouragement: understandings of a good life for children among parents and children in 3 Ethiopian communities, in J. Boyden and M. Bourdillon (eds) *Childhood Poverty: Multi-Disciplinary Approaches*, Basingstoke: Palgrave.

Camfield, Laura, Streuli, Natalia and Woodhead, Martin (2009) What's the use of 'well-being' in contexts of child poverty? Approaches to research, monitoring and children's participation, *International Journal of Children's Rights*, 17: 65–109.

Campbell, T. (2013) *In-School Ability Grouping and the Month of Birth Effect: Preliminary Evidence from the Millennium Cohort Study*, CLS Working Papers 2013/1, London: Centre for Longitudinal Studies.

Centre for Longitudinal Studies (CLS) (2007) The inter-generational transmission of disadvantage and advantage, CLS Briefings, February 2007 www.cls.ioe.ac.uk

Chakraborty, K. (2009) 'The good Muslim girl': conducting qualitative participatory research to understand the lives of young Muslim women in the bustees of Kolkata, *Children's Geographies*, 7 (4): 421–34.

Chambers, R. (1994) Participatory rural appraisal (PRA): challenges, potentials and paradigm, *World Development*, 22 (10): 1437–454.

Cheal, D. (2008) *Families in Today's World*, London: Routledge.

Children's Legal Centre (1985) Landmark decision for children's rights, *Childright*, 22: 11–18.

China.org.cn (2006) Rural women left to hold the fort at home, *China Daily*, 23 December.

Chittenden, T. (2010) Digital dressing up: modelling female teen identity in the discursive spaces of the fashion blogosphere, *Journal of Youth Studies*, 13 (4): 505–20.

Chossudovsky, M. (1997) *The Globalisation of Poverty: Impacts of IMF and World Bank Reforms*, London: Zed Books.

Christensen, P. (2002) Why more 'Quality Time' is not on the top of children's lists, *Children and Society*, 16 (1–16): 74–87.

Christensen, P. and James, A. (eds) (2008) *Research with Children: Perspectives and Practices*, 2nd edn, London: Falmer.

Christensen, P. and Mikkelsen, M. (2013) 'There is nothing here for us … !' How girls create meaningful places of their own through movement, *Children and Society*, 27 (3): 197–207.

Clarke, A. and Moss, P. (2001) *The Mosaic Approach*, London: NCB.

Cockburn, T. and Cleaver, F. (2009) *How Children and Young People Win Friends and Influence Others*, London: Carnegie Trust.

Cohen, J. (2006) Social, emotional, ethical, and academic education: creating a climate for learning, participation in democracy, and well-being, *Harvard Educational Review*, 76 (2): 201–37.

Cohen, R. and Kennedy, P. (2007) *Global Sociology*, 2nd edn, Basingstoke: Palgrave.

Cohen, R. and Kennedy, P. (2008) *Global Sociology*, 2nd edn, Basingstoke: Palgrave.

Coleman, J. and Hendry, L. (1999) *The Nature of Adolescence*, 3rd edn London: Routledge.

Collin, P. (2008) The internet, youth participation policies and the development of young people's political identities in Australia, *Journal of Youth Studies*, 11 (5): 527–42.

Community Care (2005) *How to Work in Multi-Disciplinary Teams*, 27 October. http://www.communitycare.co.uk/Articles/07/11/2005/51502/How-to-work-in-multi-disciplinary-teams.htm

Connell, R. (1987) *Gender and Power*, Cambridge: Polity.

Cook, D. (2010) The promise of an unanswered question: multi-/cross-disciplinary struggles, *Children's Geographies*, 8 (2): 221–2.

Cook, D. and Kaiser, S. (2004) Betwixt and between: age ambiguity and the sexualization of the female, *Journal of Consumer Culture*, 2 (4): 203–27.

Cooke, B. and Kothari, U. (eds) (2001) *Participation: The New Tyranny?* London: Zed Books.

Corrigan, P. (1979) *Schooling the Smash Street Kids*, Basingstoke: Macmillan.

Corsaro, W. (2011) *The Sociology of Childhood*, 3rd edn, California: Pine Forge.

Corsaro, W. and Molinari, L. (2008) Entering and observing children's worlds: a reflection on a longitudinal ethnography of early education in Italy, in P. Christensen and A. James (eds) *Research with Children: Perspectives and Practices*, 2nd edn, London: Falmer.

Cunningham, S. and Lavalette, M. (2004) 'Active citizens' or 'irresponsible truants'? School student strikes against the war, *Critical Social Policy*, 24 (2): 255–69.

Czaika, M. and de Hass, H. (2013) *The Globalisation of Migration: Has the World Really Become more Migratory?* Working Paper 68, Oxford: International Migration Institute.

Dalrymple, J. (2002) Family group conferences and youth advocacy: the participation of children and young people in family decision making, *European Journal of Social Work*, 5 (3): 287–99.

Dann, J. (1980) *The Revolution Remembered*, Chicago: University of Chicago.

Davies, M. (2008) A childish culture? Shared understandings, agency and intervention: an anthropological study of street children in northwest Kenya, *Childhood*, 5 (3): 309–30.

De Berry, J., Fazili, A., Farhad, S., Nasiry, F., Hashemi, S. and Hakimi, M. (2003) *The Children of Kabul: Discussions with Afghan Families*, USA: Save the Children.

Delphy, C. (1984) *Close to Home: A Materialist Analysis of Women's Oppression*, London: Hutchinson.

Demetrious, H., Goalen, P. and Rudduck, J. (2000) Academic performance, transfer transition and friendship: listening to the student voice, *International Journal of Educational Research*, 33: 425–41.

Denov, M. (2012) Child soldiers and iconography: portrayals and (mis)representations, *Children and Society*, 26 (4): 280–92.

Department for Children, Schools and Families (DCSF) (2007) *SEAL Guidance Booklet Secondary Schools*, London: HMSO.

— (2012) *Statutory Framework for the Early Years Foundation Stage*, London: HMSO.

Department for Education (DfE) (2011) *Letting Children be Children – Report of an Independent Review of the Commercialisation and Sexualisation of Childhood*, http://www.education.gov.uk/inthenews/inthenews/a0077662/bailey-review-of-the-commercialisation-and-sexualisation-of-childhood-final-report-published

— (2011) *The Bailey Review*, London: HMSO.

De Souza, Z. and Dick, G. (2008) Information disclosure on MySpace: the what, the why and the implications, *Pastoral Care in Education*, 26 (3): 143–57.

Deuchar, R. (2008) Seen and heard, and then not heard: Scottish pupils' experience of democratic educational practice during the transition from primary to secondary school, *Oxford Review of Education*, 34 (5): 1–18.

Dingwall, R., Eekelaar, J. and Murray, T. (1995) *The Protection of Children: State Intervention and Family Life*, 2nd edn, Oxford: Blackwell.

Donzelot, J. (1977) *The Policing of Families*, London: Hutchinson.

Dorman, P. (2008) *Child Labour, Education and Health: A Review of the Literature*, Geneva: ILO.

Driscoll, J. (2009) Prevalence, people and processes: a consideration of the implications of Lord Laming's progress report on the protection of children in England, *Child Abuse Review*, 18 (5): 333–45.

Du Bois-Reymond, M. P., Büchner, M. and Krüger, H. (1993) Modern family as everyday negotiation: continuities and discontinuities in parent–child relationships, *Childhood*, 1 (3): 87–99.

Durham, M. (2004) Constructing the 'new ethnicities': media, sexuality, and diaspora identity in the lives of South Asian immigrant girls, *Critical Studies in Media Communication*, 21 (2): 140–61.

Early Intervention Foundation (EIF) (2013) *Vision Statement* http://www.earlyinterventionfoundation.org.uk/

Eke, R., Butcher, H. and Lee, M. (eds) (2009) *Whose Childhood Is It?: The Roles of Children, Adults and Policy Makers: Children, Adults, Policy Makers?* London: Continuum.

Estrada, E. (2013) Changing household dynamics: Children's American generational resources in street vending markets, *Childhood*, 20 (1): 51–65.

Evans, G. (2006) *Educational Failure and Working Class White Children in Britain*, Basingstoke: Palgrave.

Fahey, T. (1995) Privacy and the family: conceptual and empirical reflections, *Sociology*, 29 (4): 687–702.

Fallon, P. and Tzannatos, Z. (1998) *Child Labor: Issues and Directions for the World Bank*, Washington: World Bank.

Ferchhoff, W. (1990) *West German Youth Cultures at the Close of the Eighties*, in L. Chisholm, P. Buchner, H. Kruger and P. Brown (eds) *Childhood Youth and Social Change*, London: Falmer.

Fielding, M. (2007) Beyond 'voice': new roles, relations and contexts in researching with young people, *Discourse: Studies in Cultural Politics of Education*, 28 (3): 301–10.

— (2006) Leadership, radical student engagement and the necessity of person-centred education, *International Journal of Leadership in Education*, 9 (4): 299–313.

Finkelhor, D. (2008) *Childhood Victimisation*, Oxford: Oxford University Press.

Fleer, M., Hedegaard, M. and Tudge, J. (2009) Constructing child-hood: global–local policies and practices, in M. Fleer, M. Hede-gaard and J. Tudge (eds) *Childhood Studies and the Impact of Globalisation: Practices at Global and Local Levels*, London: Routledge, pp. 1–20.

Flowerdew, J. and Neale, B. (2003) Trying to stay apace: children with multiple challenges in their post-divorce family lives, *Childhood*, 10 (2): 147–62.

Football Association (2012) *FA Proposals for the Future: Development of Youth Soccer* 13 March. http://www.keelbyunited.co.uk/blog/other/fa_proposals_for_development.html

Foster, G. et al. (1997) Factors leading to the establishment of child-headed households: the case of Zimbabwe, *Health Transition Review*, supplement to vol. 7: 155–68.

Franklin, B. (1997) The ladder of participation in matters concerning children, in J. Boyden and J. Ennew, *Children in Focus: a Manual for Participatory Research with Children*, Stockholm: Grafisk.

Fraser, N. (2000) Rethinking recognition, *New Left Review*, 3: 107–20.

Froerer, P. (2011) Children's moral reasoning about illness in Chhat-tisgarh, central India, *Childhood*, 18 (3): 367–83.

Frydenberg, E., Care, E., Freeman, E. and Chan, E. (2009) Inter-relationships between coping, school connectedness and well-being, *Australian Journal of Education*, 53 (3): 261–76.

Fyfe, A. (2007) *The Worldwide Movement Against Child Labour: Progress and Future Directions*, Geneva: ILO.

Gallagher, M. (2008) 'Power is not an evil': rethinking power in participatory methods, *Children's Geographies*, 6 (2): 137–50.

Gelles, R. (1987) *The Violent Home*, London: Sage.

— (1978) *Family Violence*, London: Sage.

Germann, S. (2006) An exploratory study of quality of life and coping strategies of orphans living in child-headed households in an urban high HIV-prevalent community in Zimbabwe, Southern Africa, *Vulnerable Children and Youth Studies*, 1 (2): 149–58.

Gerth, H. H. and Mills, C. W. (1948) *For Max Weber*, London: Routledge and Kegan Paul.

Giddens, A. (1984) *The Constitution of Society*, Cambridge: Polity.

Gilbert, R., Spatz Widom, C., Browne, K., Fergusson, D., Webb, E. and Janson, S. (2009) Child maltreatment 1: Burden and conse-quences of child maltreatment in high-income countries, *The Lancet*, 373 (9657): 68–81.

Gillies, V. (2013) From baby brain to conduct disorder: the new determinism in the classroom, Paper given at the Gender and Education Association Conference, 25 April 2013.

188   *References*

Giroux, H. (1989) *Schooling for Democracy: Critical Pedagogy in the Modern Age*, Routledge: London.

Glass, N. (1999) Sure start: the development of an early intervention programme for young children in the United Kingdom, *Children and Society*, 13: 257–64.

Goldson, J. (2006) *Hello, I am a voice, let me talk: Child Inclusive Mediation in Family Separation*, Auckland: Families Commission.

Hacking, I. (1991) The making and moulding of child abuse, *Critical Inquiry*, 17 (Winter): 253–88.

Hall, K. (1995) 'There's a time to act English and a time to act Indian': the politics of identity among British-Sikh teenagers, in S. Stephens (ed.) *Children and the Politics of Culture*, New Jersey: Princeton University Press.

Hanawalt, B. (1993) *Growing up in Medieval London*, New York: Oxford University Press.

Harris, A. (2008) Young women. Late modern politics and the participatory politics of online cultures, *Journal of Youth Studies*, 11 (5): 481–95.

Hart, J. (2008) Children's participation and international development: attending to the political, *International Journal of Children's Rights*, 16: 407–18.

— (2006) The politics of 'child soldiers', *Brown Journal of World Affairs*, 13 (1): 217–26.

— (2003) Children's clubs: new ways of working with conflict-displaced children in Sri Lanka, *Forced Migration Review*, 15: 36–9.

Hart, R. (2009) Charting change in the participatory settings of childhood: a very modest beginning, in N. Thomas (ed.) *Children, Politics and Communication*, Bristol: Policy Press.

— (1997) *Children's Participation: The Theory and Practice of Involving Young Citizens in Community Development and Environmental Care*, London: Earthscan.

Haugen, G. (2010) Children's perspectives on everyday experiences of shared residence: time, emotion and agency dilemmas, *Children and Society*, 24 (2): 112–22.

Hemming, P. and Madge, N. (2012) Researching children, youth and religion: Identity, complexity and agency, *Childhood*, 19 (1): 38–51.

Henderson, P. (2006) South African AIDS orphans: examining assumptions around vulnerability from the perspective of rural children and youth, *Childhood*, 13 (3): 303–27.

Hendrick, H. (2003) *Child Welfare: Historical Dimensions, Contemporary Debates*, Bristol: Policy Press.

— (1997) Constructions and re-constructions of British childhood: an interpretive survey, 1800 to the present, in A. James and A.

Prout (eds) *Constructing and Reconstructing Childhood*, 2nd edn, London: Falmer, pp. 34–62.

Hesketh, T., Gamlin, J. and Woodhead, M. (2006) Policy in child labour, *Archives of Diseases in Childhood*, 91 (9): 721–3.

Hetherington, M. (2003) Social support and the adjustment of children in divorced and remarried families, *Childhood*, 10 (2): 217–36.

Hevener Kaufman, N., Rizzini, I., Wilson, K. and Bush, M. (2002) The impact of global economic, political, and social transformations on the lives of children: a framework for analysis, in N. Hevener Kaufman and I. Rizzini (eds) *Globalization and Children: Exploring Potentials for Enhancing Opportunities in the Lives of Children and Youth*, New York: Kluwer Academic, pp. 3–18.

Hill, M. (2006) Children's voices on ways of having a voice: children and young people's perspectives on methods used in research and consultation, *Childhood*, 13 (1): 69–89.

Hill, M., Davis, J., Prout, A. and Tisdall, K. (2004) Moving the participation agenda forward, *Children and Society*, 18 (2): 77–96.

Hobbs, S., McKechnie, J. and Anderson, S. (2007) Making child employment in Britain more visible, *Critical Social Policy*, 27 (3): 415–25.

Hoddinott, J. (2012) Uncovering the consequences of pre-school malnutrition, in J. Boyden and M. Bourdillon (eds) *Childhood Poverty: Multi-Disciplinary Approaches*, Basingstoke: Palgrave.

Hodkinson, P. and Deicke, W. (2007) *Youth Cultures: Scenes, Subcultures and Tribes*, New York: Routledge.

Holland, S., Scourfield, J., O'Neill, S. and Pithouse, A. (2005) Democratising the family and the state? The case of family group conferences in child welfare, *Journal of Social Policy*, 34 (1): 59–77.

Hollingworth, K. (2007) Responsibility and rights: children and their parents in the Youth Justice System, *International Journal of Law, Policy and the Family*, 21 (2): 190–219.

Hood-Williams, J. (1990) Patriarchy for children: on the stability of power relations in children's lives, in L. Chisholm, P. Buchner, H.-H. Kruger and P. Brown (eds) *Childhood, Youth and Social Change*, London: Falmer.

Hooper, C. A. (2011) Child maltreatment, in J. Bradshaw (ed.) *The Well-Being of Children in the UK*, London: *Save the Children*, UK, pp. 191–212.

Hopkins, P., Olson, E., Pain, R. and Vincett, G. (2007) Mapping intergenerationalities: the formation of youthful religiosities, *Transactions of the Institute of British Geographers*, 36 (2): 314–27.

Hu, Feng (2012) Migration, remittances, and children's high school attendance: The case of rural China, *International Journal of Educational Development*, 32 (3): 401–11.

Hunleth, J. (2011) Beyond on or with: questioning power dynamics and knowledge production in 'child-oriented' research methodology, *Childhood*, 18 (1): 81–93.

Hungerland, B., Liebel, M., Liesecke, A. and Wihstutz, A. (2007) Pathways to participatory autonomy: the meanings of work for children in Germany, *Childhood*, 14 (2): 257–77.

Hur, Yongbeom and Testerman, Robin (2012) An index of child well-being at a local level in the US: the case of North Carolina counties, *Child Indicators Research*, 5 (1): 29–53.

International Labour Organization (ILO) (1999) *Convention 182*, Geneva: ILO.

— (2006) *The End of Child Labour: Within Reach, Global Report Under the Follow-Up to the ILO Declaration on the Fundamental Principles and Rights at Work*, Geneva: ILO.

— (2010) *Accelerating Action Against Child Labour*, Geneva: ILO.

— (2011) *International Programme on the Elimination of Child Labour* (IPEC), http://www.ilo.org/ipec/programme/lang–en/index. htm

Invernizzie, A. (2005) Perspectives on children's work in the Algarve (Portugal) and their implications for social policy, *Critical Social Policy*, 25 (2): 198–222.

James, A. (2009) Agency, in J. Qvortrup, W. Corsaro and M.-S., Honig (eds) *The Palgrave Handbook of Childhood Studies*, Basingstoke: Palgrave, pp. 334–45.

James, A. and Prout, A. (eds) (1997) *Constructing and Reconstructing Childhood*, 2nd edn, London: Falmer.

James, A., Jenks, C. and Prout, A. (1998) *Theorising Childhood*, Cambridge: Polity.

Jenks, C. (1982) Introduction: constituting the child, in C. Jenks (ed.) *The Sociology of Childhood: Essential Readings*, London: Batsford.

Jones, G. and Wallace, C. (1992) *Youth, Family and Citizenship*, Buckingham: Open University Press.

Joseph Rowntree Foundation (2013) *Child Poverty in the UK*. http://www.jrf.org.uk/work/workarea/child-poverty

Jupp, E. (2008) The feeling of participation: everyday spaces and urban change, *Geoforum*, 39 (1): 331–43.

Kabeer, N., Nambissan, G. and Subrahmanian, R. (2003) Needs versus rights: child labour, social exclusion and the challenge of universalising primary education, in N. Kabeer, G. Nambissan and R. Subrahmanian (eds) *Child Labour and the Right to Education in South Asia*, London: Sage.

Katz, C. (2004) *Growing up Global: Economic Restructuring and Children's Everyday Lives*, Minnesota: Minnesota University Press.

Kaufman, N. and Rizzini, I. (2002) *Globalization and Children: Exploring Potentials for Enhancing Opportunities in the Lives of Children and Youth*, New York: Springer.

Kehily, M.-J. (2012) Contextualising the sexualisation of girls debate: innocence, experience and young female sexuality, *Gender and Education*, 25 (3): 255–68.

Kendrick, M. and Kakuru, D. (2012) Funds of knowledge in child-headed households: a Ugandan case study, *Childhood*, 19 (3): 397–413.

Kenway, J. and Bullen, E. (2002) *Consuming Children: Education-Entertainment-Advertising*. Buckingham, Open University Press.

Kesby, M., Gwanyura-Ottemoller, F. and Chizororo, M. (2006) Theorising other, 'other childhoods': issues emerging from work on HIV in urban and rural Zimbabwe, *Children's Geographies*, 4 (2): 185–202.

Kim, S. and Yi, S.-H. (2010) Is privacy at risk when commercial websites target primary school children? A case study in Korea, *Children and Society*, 24 (6): 449–60.

Kimmel, C. and Roby, L. (2007) Institutionalised child abuse: the use of child soldiers, *International Social Work*, 50 (6): 740–54.

Kirby, P. and Gibbs, S. (2006) Facilitating participation: adults' caring support roles within child-to-child projects in schools and after school settings, *Children and Society*, 20 (3): 209–22.

Kitzinger, J. (1997) Who are you kidding? Children, power and the struggle against sexual abuse, in James and Prout (eds) *Constructing and Reconstructing Childhood*, London: Falmer.

Klocker, N. (2007) An example of 'thin' agency. Child domestic workers in Tanzania, in R. Panelli, S. Punch, and E. Robson, (eds) *Global Perspectives on Rural Childhood and Youth: Young Rural Lives*, New York: Routledge, pp. 83–94.

Korbin, J. (2010) Interdisciplinarity and childhood studies, *Children's Geographies*, 8 (2): 217–18.

Kraftl, P. and Horton, J. (2007) 'The health event': everyday, affective politics of participation, *Geoforum*, 38 (3): 1012–27.

Kranzl-Nagl, R. and Zartler, U. (2010) Children's participation in school and community, in B. Percy-Smith and N. Thomas (eds) *A Handbook of Children's Participation*, London: Routledge.

Kuruvilla, S., Kwan Lee, C. and Gallagher, M. (2012) (eds) *From Iron Rice Bowl to Informalization: Markets, Workers, and the State in a Changing China*, Ithica: Cornell University Press.

La Fontaine, J. (1990) *Child Sex Abuse*, Cambridge: Cambridge University Press.

Landsdown, G. (2010) The realisation of children's participation rights, in B. Percy-Smith and N. Thomas (eds) *A Handbook of Children and Young People's Participation: Perspectives from Theory and Practice*, London: Routledge, pp. 11–23.

Langer, B. and Farrar, E. (2003) Becoming 'Australian' in the global cultural economy: children, consumption, citizenship, *Journal of Australian Studies*, 27 (79): 117–26.

Lareau, A. (2011) *Unequal Childhoods: Class, Race and Family Life*, 2nd edn, University of California Press.

— (1989) *Home Advantage: Social Class and Parental Intervention in Elementary Schools*, London: Falmer.

Lasch, C. (1977) *Haven in a Heartless World: the Family Besieged*, New York: Norton.

Layard, R. and Dunn, J. (2009) *A Good Childhood*, London: Penguin.

Lee, N. (2001) *Childhood and Society: Growing Up in an Age of Uncertainty*, Buckingham: Open University Press.

Lee, N. and Motzkau, J. (2011) Navigating the bio-politics of childhood, *Childhood: A Global Journal of Child Research*, 18 (1): 7–19.

Leonard, M. (2004) Children's views on children's right to work, *Childhood*, 11 (1): 45–61.

Lewis, J. (2006) Introduction: children in the context of changing families and welfare states, in J. Lewis (ed.) *Children, Changing Families and Welfare States*, Cheltenham: Edward Elgar, pp. 1–24.

Liang, W., Hou, L. and Chen, W. (2008) Left-behind children in rural schools, *Chinese Education and Society*, 41 (5): 84–9.

Liebel, M. (2007) Opinion, dialogue, review the new ILO report on child labour: a success story, or the ILO still at a loss, *Childhood*, 14 (2): 279–84.

— (2003) Working children as social subjects: the contribution of working children's organizations to social transformations, *Childhood*, 10 (3): 265–85.

Ling, L. (2004) Cultural chauvinism and the liberal democratic order, in G. Chowdhry and S. Nair (eds) *Power, Post-Colonialism and International Relations*, London: Routledge.

Livingstone, S. (2003) Children's use of the internet: reflections on the emerging research agenda, *New Media and Society*, 5 (2): 147–66.

Livingstone, S. and Brake, D. (2010) On the rapid rise of social networking sites: new findings and policy implications, *Children and Society*, 24 (1): 75–83.

Lund, R. (2009) At the interface of development studies and child research: rethinking the participating child, in S. Aitken, R. Lund and A. Kjorholt (eds) *Global Childhoods: Globalisation, Development and Young People*, London: Routledge.

Luo, Y. (2012) Education of children left behind in rural China, *Journal of Marriage and the Family*, 74 (2): 3328–41.

Lyon, C. (2007) Interrogating the concentration on the UNCRC instead of the ECHR in the development of children's rights in England, *Children and Society*, 21 (2): 147–53.

McAdam-Crisp, J. (2006) Factors that can enhance and limit resilience for children of war, *Childhood*, 13 (4): 459–77.

Mackenzie, C. and Stoljar, N. (2000) Introduction: autonomy refigured, in C. Mackenzie and N. Stoljar (eds) *Relational Autonomy: Feminist Perspectives on Autonomy, Agency and the Social Self*, Oxford: Oxford University Press.

Maes, S., de Mol, J. and Buysse, A. (2011) Children's experiences and meaning construction on parental divorce: A focus group study, *Childhood*, 19 (2): 266–79.

Mandell, N. (1991) The least adult role in studying children, in F. Waksler (ed.) *Studying the Social Worlds of Children*, London: Falmer.

Mannion, G. (2007) Going spatial, going relational: why 'listening to children' and children's participation needs reframing, *Discourse: Studies in Cultural Politics of Education*, 28 (3): 405–20.

Mantle, G., Leslie, J., Parsons, S., Plenty, J. and Shaffer, R. (2006) Establishing children's wishes and feelings for family court reports: the significance attached to the age of the child, *Childhood*, 13 (4): 499–518.

Marson, D. (1973) *Children's Strikes in 1911*, Oxford: Ruskin College.

Mason, J. and Bolzan, N. (2010) Questioning understandings of children's participation, in B. Percy-Smith and N. Thomas (eds) *A Handbook of Children's Participation*, London: Routledge.

Matshalaga, N. and Powell, G. (2002) Editorial: Mass orphanhood in the era of HIV/AIDS, *British Medical Journal*, 324 (7331): 184–5.

Mavise, A. (2006) Child-headed households as contested spaces: challenges and opportunities in children's decision-making, *Vulnerable Children and Youth Studies*, 1 (2): 321–9.

— (2011) Child-headed households as contested spaces: challenges and opportunities in children's decision-making, *Vulnerable Children and Youth Studies*, 6 (4): 321–9.

Mayall, B. (2002) *Towards a Sociology of Childhood: Thinking from Children's Lives*, Buckingham: Open University.

— (1996) *Children, Health and the Social Order*, Buckingham: Open University Press.

Melton, G. (2002) Democratisation and children's lives, in N. Hevener Kaufman and I. Rizzini (eds) *Globalization and Children: Exploring Potentials for Enhancing Opportunities in the Lives of Children and Youth*, New York: Kluwer Academic Publishers [this is an e-book].

Meyer, A. (2007) The moral rhetoric of childhood, *Childhood*, 14 (1): 85–104.

Milbourne, L., Macrae, S. and Maguire, M. (2003) Collaborative solutions or new policy problems: exploring multi-agency partnerships in education and health work, *Journal of Education Policy*, 18 (1): 19–35.

Mitchell, T. (ed.) (2001) *Global Noise: Rap and Hip-Hop Outside the USA*, Connecticut: Wesleyan.

Mittelman, J. (1997) Restructuring the global division of labour: old theories and new realities, in S. Gill (ed.) *Globalisation, Democratisation and Multilateralism*, Basingstoke: Macmillan.

Moinian, F. (2009) 'I'm just me!' children talking beyond ethnic and religious identities, *Childhood*, 16 (1): 31–48.

— (2006) The construction of identity on the internet, *Childhood*, 13 (1): 49–68.

Montgomery, H. (2008) *An Introduction to Childhood: Anthropological Perspectives on Children's Lives*, Oxford: Wiley-Blackwell.

Moosa-Mitha, M. (2005) A difference-centred alternative to theorization of children's citizenship rights, *Citizenship Studies*, 9 (4): 369–88.

Morss, J. (1996) *Growing Critical: Alternatives to Developmental Psychology*, London: Routledge.

Moss, P. and Petrie, P. (2002) *From Children's Services to Children's Spaces*, London: Routledge Falmer.

Mount, F. (1982) *The Subversive Family*, London: Unwin.

Muncie, J. (2009) *Youth and Crime*, 3rd edn, London: Sage.

Munro, M. and Madigan, R. (1993) Privacy in the private sphere, *Housing Studies*, 8 (1): 29–45.

Murray, C. (2010) Children's rights in Rwanda: a hierarchical or parallel model of implementation, *International Journal of Children's Rights*, 18 (3): 387–403.

Naftali, O. (2010) Caged golden canaries: childhood, privacy and subjectivity in contemporary urban China, *Childhood*, 17 (3): 297–311.

Nambissan, G. (2003) Social exclusion, children's work and education: a view from the margins, in N. Kabeer, G. Nambissan and R. Subrahmanian (eds) *Child Labour and the Right to Education in South Asia*, London: Sage.

National Society for the Prevention of Cruelty to Children (NSPCC) (2011) *Premature Sexualisation: Understanding the Risks*, London: NSPCC.

Ndebele, N. (1995) Recovering childhood: children in South African reconstruction, in S. Stephens (ed.) *Childhood and the Politics of Culture*, New Jersey: Princeton University.

Neale, B. and Flowerdew, J. (2007) New structures, new agency: the dynamics of child–parent relationships, *International Journal of Children's Rights*, 15 (1): 25–42.

Nieuwenhuys, O. (1994) *Children's Lifeworlds: Gender, Welfare and Labour in the Developing World*, London: Routledge.

Nsamenang, A. (2009) Cultures in early childhood care and education, in M. Fleer, M. Hedegaard and J. Tudge (eds) *Childhood Studies and the Impact of Globalisation: Practices at Global and Local Levels*, London: Routledge, pp. 1–20.

Nyamjoh, F. (2002) Children, media and globalisation: a research agenda for Africa, in Cecilia von Feilitzen and Ulla Carlsson. *Unesco Yearbook 2002: Children, Young People and Media Globalisation*, Gothenberg: UNESCO.

Oakley, A. (1994) Women and children first and last: parallels and differences between children's and women's studies, in B. Mayall (ed.) *Children's Childhoods Observed and Experienced*, London: Falmer.

O'Connell, R. and Brannen, J. (2014) Children's food, power and control: negotiations in families with younger children in England, *Childhood*, 21 (1): 87–102.

Ogan, C. (2001) *Communication and Identity in the Diaspora: Turkish Migrants in Amsterdam and their Use of Media*, Lanham: Lexington Books.

Ohmae, K. (1990) *The Borderless World: Power and Strategy in the Inter-Linked Economy*, London: Harper Collins.

Ongay, L. (2010) Glocalists in Tijuana: youth, cultural citizenship and cosmopolitan identity, *Children's Geographies*, 8 (4): 373–80.

Orellana, M. (2001) The work that kids do: Mexican and Central American immigrant children's contributions to households and schools in California, *Harvard Educational Review*, 71 (3): 366–89.

Ortiz, I. and Cummins, M. (2011) *Global Inequality: Beyond the Bottom Billion*, Working Paper, New York: UNICEF.

Oswell, D. (2013) *The Agency of Children: From Family to Global Human Rights*, Cambridge: Cambridge University Press.

Pain, R. (2010) Ways beyond disciplinarity, *Children's Geographies*, 8 (2): 223–5.

Palmer, S. (2006) *Toxic Childhood*, London: Orion.

Parsons, T. and Bales, R. (1956) *Family Socialisation and Interaction Process*, New York: Free Press.

Parton, N. (2011) Child protection and safeguarding in England: changing and competing conceptions of risk and their implications for social work, *British Journal of Social Work*, 41: 854–75.

— (2006) *Safeguarding Childhood*, Basingstoke: Palgrave.

— (1996) The new politics of child protection, in J. Pilcher and S. Wagg (eds) *Thatcher's Children?* London: Falmer, pp. 43–60.

— (1985) *The Politics of Child Abuse*, Basingstoke: Macmillan.

Pell, K. (2010) 'No one ever listens to us': challenging obstacles to the participation of children and young people in Rwanda, in B. Percy-Smith and N. Thomas (eds) *A Handbook of Children and Young People's Participation: perspectives from theory and practice*, London: Routledge, pp. 196–203.

Percy-Smith, B. and Thomas, N. (eds) (2010) *A Handbook of Children and Young People's Participation: perspectives from theory and practice*, London: Routledge.

Peterson, M. (2005) The Jinn and the computer: consumption and identity in Arabic children's magazines, *Childhood*, 12 (2): 177–200.

Pew Social Trends (2010) The return of the multi-generational family household, *Social Demographic Trends: Pew Research Centre*, http://pewsocialtrends.org/2010/03/18/the-return-of-the-multi-generational-family-household/

Pilcher, J. (2010) What not to wear? Girls, clothing and 'showing' the body, *Children and Society*, 24 (6): 461–70.

Pinkney, S. (2011) Participation and emotions: troubling encounters between children and social welfare professionals, *Children and Society*, 25 (1): 37–46.

Pinsker, D. M., McFarland, K. and Pachana, N. A. (2010) Exploitation in older adults: social vulnerability and personal competence factors, *Journal of Applied Gerontology*, 29 (6): 740–61.

Pires, F. (2014) Child as family sponsor: an unforeseen effect of *Programa Bolsa Família* in northeastern Brazil, *Childhood*, 21 (1): 134–47.

Platt, L. (2009) *Ethnicity and Child Poverty*, London: Dept for Work and Pensions. http://dera.ioe.ac.uk/11016/1/rrep576.pdf

Pollock, D. and Van Reken, R. (2001) *Third Culture Kids: The Experience of Growing Up Among Worlds*, Boston: Nicholas Brealey.

Porter, G., Hampshire, K., Abane, A., Tanle, A., Esiah-Donkoh, K., Amoako-Sakyi, R., Agblorti, S. and Owusu, S. (2011) Mobility, education and livelihood trajectories for young people in Rural Ghana: a gender perspective, *Children's Geographies*, 9 (3–4): 395–410.

Postman, N. (1995) *The Disappearance of Childhood*, London: Comet.

Pratt, G. (2010) Listening for spaces of ordinariness: Filipino-Canadian youths' transnational lives, *Children's Geographies*, 8 (4): 343–52.

Prendergast, S. (2000) To become dizzy in our turning: body-maps and gender as childhood ends, in A. Prout (ed.) *The Body, Childhood and Society*, Basingstoke: Macmillan.

Prout, A. (2005) *The Future of Childhood*, London: Routledge Falmer.

— (2000) Childhood bodies: construction, agency and hybridity, in A. Prout (ed.) *The Body, Childhood and Society*, Basingstoke: Macmillan.

PsychoSocial Working Group (2003) *Psychosocial Intervention in Complex Emergencies: A Conceptual Framework*, Working Paper, http://www.forcedmigration.org/psychosocial/PWGinfo. htm/papers/Conceptual%20Framework.pdf

Qvortrup, J. (1994) Childhood matters: an introduction, in J. Qvortrup et al. (eds) *Childhood Matters: Social Theory, Practice and Politics*, Aldershot: Avebury, pp. 1–23.

— (2009) Childhood as a structural form, in *The Palgrave Handbook of Childhood Studies*, Basingstoke: Palgrave.

Reddy, N. (2007) Working with working children in India, in B. Hungerland, M. Liebel, B. Milne and A. Wihstutz (eds) *Working to be Someone: Child Focused Research and Practice with Working Children*, London: Jessica Kingsley.

Ridge, T. (2006) Childhood poverty: a barrier to social participation, in E. Tisdall, J. Davis, M. Hill and A. Prout (eds) *Children, Young People and Social Participation: Participation for What?* Bristol: Policy Press, pp. 23–8.

Roberts, K. (1997) Same activities, different meanings: British youth cultures in the 1990s, *Leisure Studies*, 16 (1): 1–16.

Robertson, R. (1992) *Globalization: Social Theory and Global Culture*, London: Sage.

Rosati, F. and Lyon, S. (2006) *Tackling Child Labour: Policy Options for Achieving Sustainable Reductions in Children at Work*, Geneva: UNICEF.

Rose, N. (1992) *Governing the Soul*, London: Routledge.

Rosen, D. (2007) Child soldiers, international humanitarian law, and the globalization of childhood, *American Anthropologist*, 109 (2): 296–306.

— (2005) *Armies of the Young: Child Soldiers in War and Terrorism*, New Brunswick: Rutgers University Press.

Runciman, G. (ed.) (1978) *Weber: Selections in Translation*, Cambridge: Cambridge University Press.

Rush, E. and La Nauze, A. (2006) *Corporate Paedophilia: Sexualisation of Children in Australia*, The Australia Institute, http://www.tai.org.au/documents/dp_fulltext/DP90.pdf

Ryan, K. (2012) The new wave of childhood studies: breaking the grip of bio-social dualism? *Childhood*, 19 (4): 439–52.

Rysst, M. (2010) I am only 10 years old: femininities, clothing fashion codes and the intergenerational gap of interpretation of young girls' clothes, *Childhood*, 17 (1): 76–93.

Saee, J. (2011) International investment strategy in China, in J. Saee (ed.) *China and the Global Economy*, London: Routledge.

Saith, A. and Wazir, R. (2010) Towards conceptualising child well-being in India: the need for a paradigm shift, *Child Indicators Research*, 3: 384–408.

Sayer, A. (1992) *Method in Social Science: A Realist Approach*, 2nd edn, London: Routledge.

Scholte, J. A. (2005) *Globalisation: a Critical Introduction*, Basingstoke: Palgrave.

Seedhouse, D. (1995) 'Well-being': health promotion's red herring, *Health Promotion International*, 10 (1): 61–7.

Shildrick, T. and MacDonald, R. (2006) In defence of subculture: young people, leisure and social divisions, *Journal of Youth Studies*, (9): 125–40.

Sircar, O. and Dutta, D. (2011) Beyond compassion: children of sex workers in Kolkata's Sonagachi, *Childhood*, 18 (3): 333–4.

Skelton, T. (2007) Children, young people, UNICEF and participation, *Children's Geographies*, 5 (1–2): 165–81.

Social Trends (2010) London: HMSO.

Song, Y. and Lu, H.-H. (2002) Early childhood poverty: a statistical profile, National Center for Children in Poverty, http://cpmcnet.columbia.edu/dept/nccp

Spyrou, S. (2011) The limits of children's voices: from authenticity to critical, reflexive representation, *Childhood*, 18 (2): 151–65.

Stafford, A., Laybourn, A., Hill, M. and Walker, M. (2003) 'Having a say': children and young people talk about consultation, *Children and Society*, 17 (2): 361–73.

Stasiulis, D. (2002) The active child citizen: lessons from Canadian policy and the children's movement, *Citizenship Studies*, 6 (4): 507–38.

Stephens, S. (1995) Children and the politics of culture in 'late capitalism', in S. Stephens (ed.) *Childhood and the Politics of Culture*, New Jersey: Princeton University Press.

Strelitz, L. (2004) Against cultural essentialism: media reception among South African youth, *Media, Culture and Society*, 26 (5): 625–41.

Thomas, N. (2007) Towards a theory of children's participation, *International Journal of Children's Rights*, 17: 199–218.

Thomas, N. and Percy-Smith, B. (2010) Introduction, in B. Percy-Smith and N. Thomas (eds) *A Handbook of Children and Young People's Participation: Perspectives from Theory and Practice*, London: Routledge, pp. 1–7.

Thomson, P. and Holdsworth, R. (2003) Theorising change in the educational field: re-readings of student participation projects, *International Journal of Leadership in Education*, 6 (4): 371–91.

Thorne, B. (1993) *Gender Play: Girls and Boys in School*, Milton Keynes: Open University Press.

— (1987) Re-visioning women, *Gender and Society*, March: 85–109.

Tisdall, K. (2010) Governance and participation, in B. Percy-Smith and N. Thomas (eds) *A Handbook of Children and Young People's Participation: Perspectives from Theory and Practice*, London: Routledge, pp. 318–29.

Toren, C. (2007) Sunday lunch in Fiji: continuity and transformation in ideas of the household, *American Anthropologist*, 109 (2): 285–95.

Tsegaye, S. (2009) *Orphanhood in Africa: Old Problems and New Faces*, African Child Policy Forum.

Turmel, A. (2008) *A Historical Sociology of Childhood: Developmental Thinking, Categorisation and Graphic Visualisation*, Cambridge: Cambridge University Press.

Twum-Danso, A. (2009) Reciprocity, respect and responsibility: the 3 Rs underlying parent–child relationships in Ghana and the implications for children's rights, *International Journal of Children's Rights*, 17: 415–32.

UNICEF (2006) *State of the World's Children: Childhood under Threat*, Geneva: UNICEF.

— (2013) *Child Well-Being in Rich Countries: A Comparative Overview*, Florence: Innocenti.

United Nations Educational Scientific and Cultural Organization (UNESCO) (2008) *Global Task Force on Child Labour and Education for All*. http://www.unesco.org/new/en/unesco/

United Nations (UN) (2013) *MDGs in China*, United Nations Development Programme http://www.undp.org.cn/modules.php?op=modload&name=News&file=article&catid=32&sid=6&utm_source=Revised+of+SAI+Newsletter+March+2012+-+full+version&utm_campaign=Jan+2012+newsletter+%28final%29&utm_medium=email

— (2012) *Millennium Development Goals Report 2010*, Geneva: United Nations.

— (2009) *Committee on the Rights of the Child: Report to UK*, Geneva: United Nations.

— (2008) *Committee on the Rights of the Child: Consideration of Reports Submitted by States Parties – UK*, Geneva: United Nations.

— (1989) *Convention on the Rights of the Child*, Geneva: United Nations.

United Nations Children's Fund (UNICEF) (2011) Adoption of child labour policy urged. http://www.unicef.org/bangladesh/media_4900.htm

— (2007) *Child Poverty in Perspective: An Overview of Well-Being in Rich Countries*, Florence: UNICEF Innocenti Research Centre.

— (2006a) *State of the World's Children 2007. Women and Children: The Double Dividend of Gender Equality*, Geneva: UNICEF.

— (2006b) *Children Affected by AIDS: Africa's Orphaned and Vulnerable Generations*, Geneva: UNICEF.

— (2003) *The State of the World's Children: Child Participation*, Geneva: United Nations.

Urla, J. (2001) We are all Malcolm X: Negu Gorriak, hip hop and Basque political imagery, in T. Mitchell (ed.) *Global Noise: Rap and Hip-Hop Outside the USA*, Connecticut: Wesleyan.

US Department of Education (2010) *Parent Power: Build the Bridge to Success*, Washington DC, http://www2.ed.gov/parents/academic/help/parentpower/booklet.pdf

Valentine, K. (2011) Accounting for agency, *Children and Society*, 25 (5): 347–58.

Wajcman, J. (1991) *Feminism Confronts Technology*, Pennsylvania: Pennsylvania University Press.

Wall, J. (2008) Human rights in the light of childhood, *International Journal of Children's Rights*, 16 (4): 523–43.

Watts, R. and Youens, B. (2007) Harnessing the potential of pupils to influence school development. *Improving Schools*, 10 (1): 18–28.

Weber, M. (1992 [1958]) *The Protestant Ethic and the Spirit of Capitalism*, New York: Scribner.

West, A. (2004) Children and participation: meanings, motives and purposes, in D. Crimmens and A. West (eds) *Young People and Participation: European Experiences*, Lyme Regis: Russell House.

West, A., Lewis, J. and Currie, P. (2009) Students' Facebook 'friends': public and private spheres, *Journal of Youth Studies*, 12 (6): 615–27.

Wheeler, G. (2006) Gillick or Fraser? A plea for consistency over competence in children, *British Medical Journal*, 332 (887): 1031–4.

White, S. and Choudhury, S. (2007) The politics of child participation in international development: the dilemma of agency, *The European Journal of Development Research*, 19 (4): 529–50.

Whitman, J. (2004) Two Western cultures of privacy: dignity versus liberty, *Yale Law Journal*, 113: 1151–222.

Wihstutz, A. (2011) Working vulnerability: agency of caring children and children's rights, *Childhood*, 18 (4): 447–59.

Williams, C., Edlin, J. and Beals, F. (2010) Spaces and structures: looking from the outside, in B. Percy-Smith and N. Thomas (eds) *A Handbook of Children and Young People's Participation: Perspectives from Theory and Practice*, London: Routledge, pp. 287–90.

Williams, S. and Williams, L. (2005) Space invaders: the negotiation of teenage boundaries through the mobile phone, *Sociological Review*, 53 (2): 314–31.

Willis, P. (1977) *Learning to Labour*, Aldershot: Avebury.

Woldehanna, T., Tefera, B., Jones, N. and Bayrau, A. (2005) *Child Labour, Gender Inequality and Rural/Urban Disparities*, Young Lives http://www.dfid.gov.uk/r4d/PDF/Outputs/YoungLives/wp20-execsummary.pdf

Woodhead, M. (1999) Combating child labour: listen to what the children say, *Childhood*, 6 (1): 27–50.

Woodhouse, B. B. (2009) The courage of innocence: children as heroes in the struggle for justice, *University of Illinois Law Review*, 5: 1567–90.

World Health Organisation (WHO) (2013) *Global Health Observatory*, http://www.who.int/gho/child_health/mortality/neonatal_infant_text/en/index.html

— (2012) *World Conference on Social Determinants of Health: Fact File on Health Inequities* http://www.who.int/sdhconference/background/news/facts/en/

Wyness, M. (2013) Global standards and deficit childhoods: the contested meaning of children's participation, *Children's Geographies*, 11 (3): 340–53.

— (2012) *Childhood and Society*, 2nd edn, Basingstoke: Palgrave.

— (2009a) Adults' involvement in children's participation: juggling children's places and spaces, *Children and Society*, 23 (6): 395–406.

— (2009b) Children representing children: participation and the problem of diversity in UK youth councils, *Childhood*, 16 (4): 535–52.

— (2003) Children's space and interests: constructing an agenda for student voice, *Children's Geographies*, 1 (2): 223–39.

— (2001) Children, childhood and political participation: case studies of young people's councils, *International Journal of Children's Rights*, 9: 193–212.

— (1999) *Contesting Childhood*, London: Falmer.

Xiang, B. (2007) How far are the left-behind left behind? A preliminary study in rural China, *Population, Space and Place*, 13: 179–91.

Yao, J. and Mao, Y. (2008) Rural left-behind children's academic psychology in Western China and the school management countermeasures, *Frontiers of Education in China*, 3 (4): 535–46.

Yeung, H. (1998) Capital, state and space: contesting the borderless world, *Transactions of the Institute of British Geographers*, 32 (3): 291–309.

Zeiher, H. (2003) Shaping daily life in urban environments, in P. Christensen and M. O'Brien (eds) *Children in the City: Home, Neighbourhood and Community*, London: Routledge Falmer, pp. 66–81.

Index